CW00818834

THE BOOK OF BARUCH BY THE GNOSTIC JUSTIN

GEOFFREY HILL

The Book of Baruch by the Gnostic Justin

EDITED BY
Kenneth Haynes

OXFORD
UNIVERSITY PRESS

OXFORD
UNIVERSITY PRESS

Great Clarendon Street, Oxford, OX2 6DP,
United Kingdom

Oxford University Press is a department of the University of Oxford.
It furthers the University's objective of excellence in research, scholarship,
and education by publishing worldwide. Oxford is a registered trade mark of
Oxford University Press in the UK and in certain other countries

First Edition published in 2019

Impression: 2

Published in the United States of America by Oxford University Press
198 Madison Avenue, New York, NY 10016, United States of America

British Library Cataloguing in Publication Data
Data available

Library of Congress Control Number: 2018952858

ISBN 978–0–19–882952–2

Printed and bound by
CPI Group (UK) Ltd, Croydon, CR0 4YY

This is that Saturnine time of the year which most molesteth such splenetick Bodies (as mine is) by the revolution of melancholick blood, which throweth up fastidious fumes into the head, whereof I have had of late my share:

HENRY WOTTON (1568–1639)

Who can discern those planets that are oft *Combust*, and those stars of brightest magnitude that rise and set with the Sun, untill the opposite motion of their orbs bring them to such a place in the firmament, where they may be seen evning or morning.

JOHN MILTON (1608–1674)

Plato banishd Poets out of his Republique, and yet forgot that that very Commonwealth was merely Poeticall.

SAMUEL BUTLER (1613–1680)

Whether the ignominious death of Arius in a boghouse was not a story feigned and put about by Athanasius above twenty years after his death?

ISAAC NEWTON (1642–1727)

Qu. W^t becomes of the *aeternae veritates? Ans.* They vanish.

GEORGE BERKELEY (1685–1753)

CONTENTS

The Book of Baruch
by the
Gnostic Justin

1

Rehearse the autopsy. Psyche cut as ever. Not clever. Cute, my arse.

Gross the antennae of abstruse *monnaie*. Grand Opera phoney, did you say?

Nascent fissures; indecent pressures; thong askew; thing into thing; I ask you.

Unpleasant sly origins barely decent. Brythonic goddess of panic still on the
  margins. Explains my odes.

Tone of address enough to amaze even that amazonian crone Tough Shit.
  Genius does mean us, I guess. Confess to what Swift & Co. termed a
  'bite'. Absolutely nothing to consummate, though, as yet.

Blitz fire-squalls. St Bride's bells shout, fall about, for an hour; tower splits
  its sides.

The axe-head shifts on its haft. In Thaxted the stag's tines tread to strange
  tunes under the red flags.

2

Entertain me to the six fingers of your left hand; your collar of esses joined
  by the ampersand; your house near the Minoresses; 'inner qualities' *v.*
  inequalities; the doubtful liberties of your mind.

What laws do they compose? What does the judgement comprise? No need
  to respond in blood. But: debate the good nature of the city-state, that
  odd creature.

A stilted conversation on behalf of a jilted nation defaulted.

'High philosophy' well uninformed. How formidably they die, *them'd*, or not
  even so hymned.

No care to get the voice out there anymore. Thought mere noise.

'Those harmless Guy Fawkes sparklers which terrified me, aged two, three;
  from which I fled with screams.'

St Lawrence Jewry, fat organ pipes aroast, bells falling and bawling, gave up
  the ghost, evanesced on the spot.

Whitbread's Brewery, near the old Grub Street site, did not.

Entertain me to your antiphon.

3

Thrice-refused thesis. The Word in Crisis. Serious judgement absurd.
Fresh from your brain the wren as dinosaur.
Conserve energy; enrage no nerve; deploy the curve. Preserve, not trample,
      the pieties.
Funds ample; needs simple.
Fix car; detox malign cosine. Do tax. Cry pax.

4

Took a vow. Did I text you about it? And how!
The mouth that has sucked dribbles with usufruct of pebbles forthwith.
These are not notes that get nowhere but safe shots that misfire a lot.
The Holborn Empire itself will sing on its pyre, relapse to clay and air.
A desire to applaud everything on the high wire is not good. My ears ring.
Gone too far too fast at the new rate. Retriangulate on the London Stone.

5

The last august praise-singer, sin-eater, rain-bringer plucked from the planet.
      'Friends "aghast"; sacred tripod in jeopardy.'
Raise finger. Renounce a degree of anger. File a dead ringer.
When necessary refill with 'Swan' that handsome accessory your 'Pickwick'
      fountain pen.
The curious technologies of the Logos, now thought mere curiosities rather
      than curios, long since laid awkwardly to rest at Weeping Cross:
Rest. Return the eyes to what they apprise best. Do not mourn.
Discommode all too human nature with the goad. *Jedermann* to feature as a not
      entirely travestied creature.

6

Sir Aylmer Firebrace, determined of face, in a state of grace, striding the dark;
    chief surveyor of the Blitz: people dead in the seats of night's vast
    cinema, struck by percussive shock, transfixed by the main feature's
    repetitive showing, glowing block by block.
Raymond Gram Swing and Ed Murrow transmitting London's courage and
    sorrow with solemn zing.
Stuart Hibberd broadcasting from a cupboard; Bruce Belfrage, whose apology
    for that bomb did not seem absurd at the time.
Neither did the King's Speech nor Churchill hammering on about a long stretch.
Absurdity was still your favourite, very well paid, East End music hall kvetch.

7

Len Rosoman in Shoe Lane. Write on that if you can.
One man pressed flat as a skate: even his tin hat.
It was, I hope, quick; not like that woman in Tudor York who kept her soul
    tidy—a good Catholic lady—and met with things dark, shapeless,
    inhuman, in the midst of the everyday and things common.
Traumatized Rosoman. *Dulle Griet* (Brueghel) maybe did haul him out.
We can pray for that, even those of us not methodically devout.

8

Things are now calmer, would you agree, Sir Aylmer? The dome of the rock
    amid fiery smoke, a work of instantaneous art, immortal, apart.
Instinct is genius, as Kit Smart almost said.
Whitbread, house of Whitbread, standing in for the City, a substantial piety, so
    some would claim: the veritable Elohim, ensconced a little northward of
    that vast flame laying all to waste.
You can mime only so much variety of pity for what is past.
It is not, I insist, a test of reluctant shame re-investing an old womb.

9

Dulle Griet—Mad Meg—do grandly highlight her through a bad fug.

Up on your fool feet. Play tough. She's lumpen, it's said; that Arnolfini's bride would do well to avoid.

If she's not in pursuit she's nonetheless hot-foot. 'Dulle Griet with her loot', so it has been put.

Either that or the 'scant possessions' of prurient intercessions, observations of irrelevant cant which I have had to invent.

If Rosoman were not now dead he would be one hundred and one.

Wall falling on two firemen in Shoe Lane. I admire the beautiful curved plane. Years of mental pain were not what he deserved.

10

If St Paul's had gone, not to be made immortal in the photo epiphany of that December night, the City reduced to a mere hallucinatory dome of red-umbers peppered with embers, loud with falling bell-chambers, a scorching mire (as indeed it was): would that have finished us, however much the Old Man admonished us? No. We were then a spiritual people revering a spirited Wren steeple albeit in a downcast thumbs-up way. Unsteepled if need be.

Vichy peace was unfathomable malign Cathay where a vicious naked emperor held sway in his robes of device.

11

Whitbread, house of Whitbread, since you were left standing, I must employ you as a stand-in, though Tate and Lyle might do just as well; for I require the sweetly comestible, whether or not through-scoured by fire. The dead lion with his bees disturbed me at three and four. Beer was a let-out sour-sweet odour caught in passing a pub's closed door.

What was it I so cheaply bought, so simple-mindedly wrought: mingling sound always, it seemed, a mystic fairground, the clash-cling of cash-register registered only as a strange raw thing?

One goldfish with mange—a Brummie ragman's scam—was, then, my worst encounter with things that estrange.

('He can't be serious?' 'As the wind veers, he is. He even says, "externalize as the best substitute for becoming wise." ')

12

Bless Mr Whitbread, virtue-accoutred. Is enterprise no longer a term of
high praise?

In nineteen twenty 'a new spray gun invention' gets a mention.

'Spray can' is belated; not by me much rated, though I'm out of touch.

'Spray tower', given as nineteen thirty-seven, breeds metamorphosis of steel,
feeds what you feel about power and crisis.

Yeats and von Hügel, no longer quite so regal, but still 'tracing mazes' like
hare and beagle.

13

That Brythonic goddess of panic: I need to hear more of her.

Panic is as close as most of us get to fear.

I've known just the one automatic panic-attack from the auto-chthonic, plus a
fair whack of aftershock; and have since travelled from fair to fair, a freak
of commonplace with smirk and grimace.

14

Reith had retired, not universally admired, though, in my own Pantheon, there
together with Everyman's tragic son.

Electrical interference still led them a merry dance: an anxious glance at every
appliance.

Orthodoxy to make you wince.

'Tight shoes' I would still have entitled every trim announcer; or even 'cherry
bum', the term borrowed from a nickname of the Crimean lancer—
though by no means the same as 'lackey of the régime'; perhaps more
like dispatchful jockey: such would be my theme.

The mike was not impartial during the General Strike.

15

This international finance, more vicious even than Vichy France to the world's
    well-being; that is not for de Gaulle's freeing, nor Simone Weil's, nor
    Queen Wilhelmina's nor the Nine Bright Shiners.

Not by the fifty unseaworthy destroyers and other poor stayers, not by those
    pitiable tanks for which the Reds gave us grudged thanks despite our
    sacrificial trouble in shipping them at all in fragile convoys that appal.
    Not by any roll-call of generous keepers and weepers.

That archaic realm, holding us to our place, could, it is true, ultimately benefit
    the human race: all too trashable film of someone demotic yet noble
    at helm.

Voice-over of the celebrity retriever.

Eagle-eyed ancient history, look down on us from your eyrie with resolved
    countenance: as when, in the *Daily Mail*, I read about Spain, and drew
    dread in, and put the question 'will it come here?' to my dad who 'never'
    replied though he knew well it would.

A dense wake spins behind us and we glimpse mountains.

16

In St Giles, Cripplegate ('tower without steeple') itself a blitz-cripple with
    random bits remaining ('few fittings survived the war'), Milton's bust
    came well out of the blast.

God bless us, everyone; save us from idolatry and false pride.

I do not think we are fated; nor did Milton, though his politics never caught on.

17

Each of Milton's London houses is well-known, though of his remnanted
    body there is none.

He too for a time housed in the Barbican. Did his tomb in St Giles vanish
    before the bomb?

Rumour painted full of tongues dissipates his rights and wrongs; his belongings,
    his earthly state, attenuate into disparate things.

This is so often what energy or lethargy brings; at times requiring jet mourn-
    ing rings and the like: better than one's head on a spike, which could
    have been Milton's last stroke of bad luck.

But I repeat: luck is not fate.

18

Son of one who was moneywise; yet ever a novice of losses; never a hope to
 recoup. There was always something up.
Latterly, led by the hand in his good grey coat, a blind good looker, looking like
 a Quaker.
The verse canonized by Addison's bland-minded *jus*, modified to suit a caste
 taste in beauties, alas.
Truer by far was Johnson's animus.
And of course Will Blake gave him a good crack as Muse.
I would be slow to advise where and when justice lies.
High poetry is another name for the lottery.

19

Immortality may be a good morning's work. But to someone with rare luck,
 knock-knock.
Problems with subsidence, as like as not, three times in ten.
The list of Wren churches restored post-Blitz is heartening.
Though one must adjust to temporal foreshortening, it is better than derelict
 sentiment's outreach, the *War Requiem*, advanced by shellshocked loud-
 speakers, with wreckers moving in on the 'great Calm', if not at this time
 the Great Wen.

20

The Commonwealth shilling is no longer mine, and I repine.
Cromwell seized the estate; it became barely a protectorate. Many will differ
 on this with an old duffer.
Best and worst we shit poison and befoul our prison.
Somebody has proof, could demonstrate (*whoof!*), that a Tudor cess-pit may
 contain methane; could floor a fit man who has pickaxed the lid. Read
 Jonson, that great rat-retriever, regarding the Fleet river, or Donne on
 the stink in his study.
Bravo, the high sick melancholy, merchant venturers, posturers in skin-tight
 theology, epoch-equipping poets at it like stoats. Bravo, everybody!
There is no solitude proportionate to solitary pride. It is audiences that must
 judge nuances. Even so, contend that there's yet a secure legendary
 command, a hierarchy of visitation, a sphere of pure metaphysical fire
 signing-off on the nation.

21

A Song for the Lord Mayor's Table, composed while Walton was still compos
and able (sing the bells of Whitechapel to the Bishop of London and the
Dean of St Paul's), reveals that privilege is by extension equitable;
though equity was not native to the City and has been, on occasion,
ejected from the Mansion House.

The virtuous utility of art resides—presides—in proximities held magnetically
apart. To compose to a rare standard an *amuse-gueule* for five hundred or
more at a dull feast without taste is to strike an elective chord of affinity,
amid the mêlée of public mood, with those whom the keepers of power
rise ordained to exclude.

Royal Tudor satyr masks, with horns and tusks worn down to papier-mâché
husks conserved, or not, at Hampton Court, are revelled-in by those
who would maintain our nation's token place—even now, without
grace—in the Divine Plan.

22

The City was destroyed through torpor and oversight though few even now
will admit that; and become shifty and annoyed.

Its real destroyers were the employers: offices to which none had keys during
the weekend break when incendiaries struck. Employees behaved well,
challenged the burning wall with ridiculous stirrup pump and pail.

The Cathedral Church of St Paul was upheld by its own grandly ordained
soul, believe that who will. I speak as a fool.

St Giles, Cripplegate, now stands as icon to the Barbican Estate.

And something of England's real polity is part of the realty.

Milton's 'noble and puissant nation' not even a begged notion.

'A very decent interment' he had. Excuse me a moment.

23

'Vis inertiae is false', said Kit Smart, who said also 'Newton was wrong'.
Madness is posthumously useful, though not so accommodating as song.

Ill luck's one eye is beady and stays steady.

Newtonian physics is outmoded; Kit was unjustly offloaded.

No-one greatly minds the lack of amends. 'I'd as lief pray...' is your average
take-away.

Some deep poets are like divers with the bends.

24

Those who poetaste are not like novices at the *piste*, learning how to coordinate
  brain, knee, wrist. To me, they present themselves as a despised caste,
  breeding on, off, their own waste; ignorant as to why wreaths of myrtle
  and laurel invest Milton's bust.
Who say 'cordiality responsible for such uncongeniality'? (*Psst!* Paul Klee.)

25

The planets that combust in their own dust and yet revive as we believe they
  must; the intellective spheres' sublime account that we find words for
  since we must invent: Mercator of the stars and hemispheres and the
  just wars; and subcreator even of our own stature in the arena of
  nature—
I would have prayed to excel in mathematics and music if I had prayed at all;
  envying Wren and the musicians of the Chapel Royal; passacaglias and
  Purcell; for that is where the mind stands to itself, albeit in hell.
No, not in hell. Immediately I am airlifted away from this well-balanced
  domain on the near side of oblivion or ultimate pain.
I am found amid rough paragraphs. How will this move the seraphs who affect
  the spheres as a form of superior pastime? We shall miss time, I fear; and
  the significance of musical cadence and grammatical tense.
All the same, mathematical dyslexia is real: like the tax year and the need for
  caveat, a true consequence of the Fall.
It shuts us out of a great part of our mind's estate.
Restitution is the burden of what I am about.
There's talk of whales magnifying a human cry when they are struck and
  dying. It is unedifying. Grief and shame run amok. Mock tears? The
  stars do not fall; they appear to blur and swell.

26

John Milton senior a transubstantiation denier as I idly suppose; not one
   wilfully to deform the deiform as he would see it. Grand deity of the
   spirit—trust him to declare it. No devotee of the Sacred Heart.
   Precursor of John Bunyan? Need I continue?

But not one of the poorer brethren on God's breadline.

He could, at any rate, assure benefits for his son; and kept things well in tune,
   to the tune of 'York' which he harmonized in a good four square block,
   as it is sung to this day.

The Minster carillon now carries the melody which, I believe, displeases
   nobody. The tourists hear it and look up; the towers, seemingly animated,
   rear back then swoop.

27

A rose-head's shape, wind-burled, wryed at the nape, shows there as crimped
   and wan, as new skin to a wound. Sentiment flourishes; it is familiar
   ground.

Few trees appear more splinter-bare than the fig tree in winter. In England,
   that is. It gives notice.

Poetry is no less moving an oratory. And I care about that and take time out to
   grieve, and feel shame, and so on, in the commination season.

Vastness of Chinese wealth; miniature Vale of Health. Alienate, Keats lies
   sleeping Italianate.

Xu Pei Wing is not weeping, for us or our ill-keeping.

28

Was Clare never the worse for malaria? Kit Smart was no hoodlum, however
   much he took Bedlam to heart.

Dryden was not a drunkard, though doubtless he could drink hard in the mode
   of the time. He retained his sound ear for rhyme. He would have gone
   off lithium in order to reclaim rhythm.

Regret no quinine at the edge of Peterborough Great Fen, though there was
   opium which did some a good turn.

29

Had I lived when you lived in Barbican, or perhaps ages before then,
    Shittebowrelane would have been briefly my domicile, John.
I would have passed through, let us say, though not as a jesting stoic.
You were heroic in your day and had great style.
How might I have been measured against your ruthless truth? You cannot now
    sound me; but then you would not have found me. I would not have
    hailed you; I would not have crossed the waste ground, vile as I was,
    violently to be reviled.
Imagination's Milton is not Milton nor is it Milton's imagination.
In limbo abide the Tyger, the huger crustacean, the shorter-lived denizens of
    Shittebowrelane.

30

Complex the issues, even the simple issues of blood; not entirely understood
    within the parameters of metred gravity.
Pondus not any more clinching depravity. *Nefas* goes SatNav on TV among the
    vanities.
Nominate an aegrotat the highest order of state beyond words. Have it fought
    over, even by lover with lover, in the Great Court of Surds, with hate.
Those severe gnostics have us there, you must concede and admire, up top
    with sex and acrostics.
Did you truly find Newton on Gravity abstruse? I thought he hit the button.
    Await your reply, but not eagerly.
And let us have the thriving clove gillyvor stand in for the love of truth.

31

If twice last century the working class was betrayed, as Frank Musgrove said,
    first by the breaking of the General Strike; next, when the grammar
    schools were disbanded, small wonder the national competence is now
    stranded and barely lexic; if not worse: labouring with curses, as our bat-
    tle cruisers in the Great War—O deviser of similitudes—failed under
    fire and went to blazes. And 'brilliant' is a word of lament for those too
    early dead; as once in the Ypres Salient so now by anorexic suicide,
    obesity and the jihad.

32

As, with the draining of summer, shadows bleed and spread, at first scarcely
heeded (and to add 'I am now eighty-two' sounds a shade twee) you
decide for the house, drawing with you the shadow of a muse; and must
re-acclimatize to indoors, everything in slow spin, the cold obstructive
stove with nothing in; and maybe tweak from oblivion that indispensable
throwaway phrase which is a revelation and no surprise.

33

Not precisely Baruch by the book, a nation's inclinations to get pissed and to
defile luck.

Trade me the name of him who tried pre-emptive requiem for a degraded
realm.

Unbelievable the credible reality of wealth, entitlement and open stealth:
London's wag-bishop, his eulogy to pâté during a funeral of state not
judged a mishap.

'The swine ran into the midst of the waters and perished there' (*after*
Winstanley, but the Bible mainly).

34

A Neil Gaiman-inspired puppet fantasy about Prince Rupert and the Winter
Queen: it is, my dear, as if we had never been; and I am scared.

The clever ablative dead keep watch from way ahead.

Ben Jonson, John Dee, Inigo Jones: I would entertain them for a short solstitial
day, though not all three at once.

Coke, house of Coke, you wrote a Shakespearean book about justice; though,
for that, others paid the price. You were a brute at assize: recusants made
render to deep mortal shock, strewn across and around the quartering
block. Let it end soon.

London caught, rapt, in matt ice above the Bridge, is forever on edge about its
dark ménage.

Its metaphysics, conspiratorial analogues, move under majestic leagues of
winter thunder.

35

Whether it's in meticulous detail of prevailing weather that sanity presides,
    I cannot readily say. Saneness is shifty and becomes a particular hard-
    ness. Such guardedness is well cast when it performs citizen's arrest on
    its own house leerers and liars; empowers, tracking their black spoors,
    all those who have been struck by real lightning indoors.
Clare, house of Clare, how beautifully the name twice takes its place here.
In his madness he fancied himself ennobled and mightily fabled.
Humiliation does not possess even its own proper haunt of distress, its
    memorial audition; its cenotaph the waste cost of the nation in the
    process, the press, of common affront.

36

Like much else rebuilt out of brick dust, ash, and silt of soot; a holocaust in
    that word's true cast: a multiplex burnt offering, residue of scorched
    hollows, roast flesh, hallows torched, when the City went up.
Roman and Saxon roused from half-houseled sleep where they had housed.
The font cover here a static fountain of detail divinely stressed.
All Hallows Barking: let her take precedence in this litany and purview of holy
    residence; saint-neighboured neighbourhood, its subterrane of the
    uncanny; and lost detritus of the not to be doubted many who were tried
    in faith, who stood forth for one truth or another, of whom no record
    survives in the decommissioned hives of ecclesiastical and common law,
    but of whom some 'noble essences'—Thomas Browne—remain.
....

St Andrew Holborn for some years appeared woe-begone, as did other Wren
    masterworks after Blitz drama and trauma.
St Mary Abchurch, for example, that intricate reredos torn into two thousand
    bits, grieved for, retrieved by sublime near-microscopic sleights, reset as
    if the miraculous were simple.
Burning St Mary-le-Bow, in ravishing show, saluted by her own bells, a last
    cascade of thrashing, mangled squeals as down they go.
St Margaret Pattens: she came through it in better state. We should not spiel
    the less well of her for that.
St Andrew Undershaft is home to the tomb of John Stow. He is shown stuck
    patiently with his craft, the writer's perpetual motion requital of things
    sedulously or by chance bereft.
....

St Mildred, Bread Street: good craftsmen in stone, lead, wood, characteristically employed.

Where Shelley and Mary Wollstonecraft's daughter were wed, notwithstanding his opinion of God.

St Mildred, Bread Street: of that small fine interior nary a sign. All dead and buried. All gutted and gone.

Nineteen hundred and forty-one.

....

The bishops destroyed more Wren churches than the Blitz did. But not well-adorned, well-husbanded St Bride.

Incendiaries overrode sacred boundaries; were caddish and delivered: fireworks at first snapped magnesium-white; afterwards took hold, grew black-reddish, unfurled, stood forth in dark flagrant gold.

Water carried to the spot in a tin hat or by a Heath Robinson machine proclaimed ingenuity, courage, and 'an unquenchable spirit of fun'.

Sand was more effective than water, as by belated directive. Neither available against that wind, the first fire-storm of pan-Germania's multi-hecatomb. Or did Warsaw grab that claim? Or Coventry? Or Rotterdam?

It is permissible to be grieved for intricate carved woodwork that could not be saved. Grief lacks the cultural aura of Pity, to which Blake once gave short shrift and which has so endowed and enriched Coventry city.

Pathos is not faith. Coventry's ruin merited rebuilding and restoration stone by stone; as in Europe they have indeed done so many times.

It ought not to have remained, a perpetual reproach to those destructively inclined, like a medieval pool—say, a bone-dry St Winifred's Well—that Alice's retaliatory weeping could never fill.

....

We have the right saint even though the right address seems a bit quaint.

St Nicholas Cold Harbour alias St Nicholas Cole Abbey: you also have suffered dereliction, which yields returns of scorn on unction which may be proffered.

Some say the City is ill-devoted, prizes its livery halls, enriches guild churches; deals out Dick Whittington's bequests.

Generous in its own house, it is a place of trysts and has been well-narrated in ample carvery:

'The high dome of Paul's', so full of history's whispers and rumours it both shrills and is sonorous.

....

Moving within the light gravity of that grave planet the moon—

Providing the odd detail to the body of the whole, a younger Hawksmoor to an old Wren, even though you also are an old man.

Early circuits become a rotunda or a *mappa mundi* without Jerusalem at its centre but encircled by the 'chartered Thames' in an unmistakeable loopiness.

One becomes a flat earther, a joke, for the rediscovering of a lost nation, for a regeneration of divine themes, a gnostic hierarchy of poems that, even so, may not 'take' as in certain prophetic passages of Blake.

The first 'Holy Thursday' was aired by Obtuse Angle in the house of Steelyard the Lawgiver; an unlikely muse, an unpropitious delivery, which is how genius is declared in the ideal dystopia.

If I have ever known a poetics it is this.

I refuse your thesis of simple catharsis.

The real Jerusalem is a many times defused and re-instated bomb.

I close my eyes; open them again; I remain an old man with a young brain.

. . . .

Unless of course it's the worsening Blitz and the burning tower is doing the splits: filmed-falling metaphor once more, as the toppling creel of half-melted bell-metal, astonishing collocations of syntax and semiotics, enjoys its slow-motion tricks, stayed ultimate unreel, luxuriating in the wondrous peal which some near-death veteran will shakingly recall to that final interviewer from hell, or to no-one at all.

(Whereas, in fact, those big-belled towers, St Bride, St Mary-le-Bow, St Lawrence Jewry, were gutted but not felled; post-war, resealed and refitted, take up again the story to the telling of which they are so well suited.)

The garments of the wise are parted among the self-connivers. Clever us, many will say. Angular articulation may indicate sanity. The demented redo endless variants of the monotonous.

To catch our public speech 'at it', with weeping debauch seeming to define the state, hysteria, womb-emptying 'by definition', the upended and shaken long-emptied pouch of the bespoken: this you would need to narrate.

Thirties jazz which, unheard, I declared crude, sounds proud and austere to me now; accurate music appropriate to heaven. Some may say, even so, that I blaspheme. Let them.

37

Chesterton's unalloyed joy in describing the national genius displayed by
     Trabb's boy in *Great Expectations* as part of the entire polyphony, weav-
     ing its own strand in the web of the mind's making, is at once grand and
     heartbreaking: because whatever it was, whatever was done in its name,
     is gone; and we are alone, measuring from within the dimension of a
     stone but less equipped than a toad to endure with nothing there but a
     set stare of loathing.
'Does it have in its head a great garnet as yet undisplayed?' could be asked by
     any child reasonably well-read, though the prissy locution is all mine.
Dimension, dispensation, and the like, are compoundings of good measure.
     Neither you nor I, I think, ever brought them to such a stone of seizure;
     and 'open, sesame!' is yet another cry of shame.

38

Symbolism is not all cake and spiders and rage-embalmed wedding day
     widders. 'Beggar him', commandingly pleaded Miss Havisham. It is a
     terrific theme. Perhaps it is the 'general balm' wherewith all negatives
     finally affirm.
Creation is loss, I will happily affirm that; a scarcely felt re-adjustment on
     another planet. In a thousand years someone will remark upon it: intrin-
     sic value and the ever more remote sphere of capital gains.
Eternity is in particulars that exclude pity? No-one explains. Unimaginable
     lines may survive in mineral veins. Repetitiousness of the mute wherein
     lie the odes of state.
Symbolism is and is not codes. What say we take urgently to the roads, fluently
     riding the camber, in good time to re-arrive at the fragilely self-engrossed
     wedding chamber?

39

Newton was a type of gnostic, I suspect; one of a one-man sect.

His theology was less Logos than complex acrostic with the power to vex.

For so it goes.

Let us meet for the last time in the great Porter Tun Room of Whitbread's
Brewery in Chiswell Street: Ernest the Policeman, Mr Growser, Larry
the Lamb; Sir Isaac also, secure in his fame, Plumian Chaired, an
inspired choice.

My last guest I would repose less trust in: Anon, author of *The Book of Baruch
by the Gnostic Justin*. This is not Wren though it might once have been.

Is porter any better for you than gin?

The spirit of the age is not now even its notorious road rage, but is stuck some-
where between Aylesbury rapper and Tupperware.

I mourn any gifted old man, 'a pelican and a nest in copper' on his now
unmused notepaper; his final will undrafted, still in denial.

40

Albeit the creative will is claustral to the point where it goes postal (US), as it
often does, it is amazing how much my late reasonable style appears to
derive from the Gnostic Bible, which I wish I knew better.

The serendipitous many times deceives with its priorities.

A malign form of serendipity at large has for long run through the City, where
impetus is violent anarchic discharge, a primitive gunpowder train set
sizzling by Anon.

Enter John Donne with his 'melancholy hat', at need to put things right
with *Devotions upon Emergent Occasions* and creed and credence, none of
which is much rated here in the deflated hemisphere where intrinsic
value will never be taken into its true milieu and our grandest poetics
perform their mystic dance of savagely disputed provenance.

41

'Conferring with a close captive in a strange tongue' is a cogent job descrip-
tion. The man who discerned this had in mind Newgate or the Fleet
or Little-Ease; and an irruption of faith-to-death, or, of being self-
estranged, like, brain-damaged, only worse, damned.
Byrd almost always preferred to set the lamenting or the protesting Word;
interspersed with protestations to the Virgin Protectress of the Lost, and
to the Holy Ghost.
I'm not sure which variant I like best, or if I like any.
They break you out of yourself and sneak you into yourself at the same hear-
ing. They are uncanny and unsparing; adopt the ramifications of the
abrupt to proclaim and defame the passions in their harsh profusions.
This is how great poetry understands the adept.

42

Grub Street is now Milton Street; its humiliation is complete: one of the
laughables in the neighbourhood of Sam Whitbread's stables where the
Lord Mayor's heavy-set, heavily insured, state coach is politely stored.
In the grand Porter Tun Room the Word is heard from and response is for hire;
but I am not there; nor is Larry the Lamb, I fear.
Poems on the Underground has gone ultrasound and state of the art; and he has
been belatedly found not to have a heart.

43

Dealing as I have to with the destructive aspects of stress, I confess to what
I find appealing: Vanbrugh, for instance, at once rough and master of a
grand elegance. Or not: indebted to others, it was said, for matters pro-
portional; who was what botanists have termed a 'sport', aestheticists
may describe as 'gauche', 'eccentric'; but who, in a clown-with-fiddle
way, could hold countervalent series and stresses at play in stone and on
stage; who did not appear to grudge the world or encounter despair,
though how can I judge? There was a public detritus of fear: of civil war,
of bankruptcy and abuse. I doubt he was religious or religiose.
The stratum into which I would have been born was not a desideratum.
He might have pitched me a coin, had I held his horse at an inn.

44

Timon's poet, if for brevity's sake I may call him that, enjoys the rich man's wine and fruit and cake; and speaks well of all, as if by contract. He is a competent rogue, right for a satirical prologue, or an entr'acte or a *thé dansant*.

Timon's Villa is tragedy's vaudeville. Timon or Apemantus should be played by Max Miller. I would play both myself if I still sought fame and did not have eighty-two years to my name.

To handle Timon's curse even now calls for lemon juice and a candle.

45

There is a claw in civility and the civil that plays the very devil.

If in the mood it can draw blood with grace before food.

Pity is sacred touchstone for one who is scared and would evade question.

Dulle Griet will pick something up and run with it, from ruin to ruin.

I am glad not to have seen what she had—not at first hand, I mean.

We are largely depraved by the small screen.

And spurious Pity, lathering her spurs, scatters small favours of curiosity to the laity.

46

Only once have I exited a theatre midway: a brutish impropriety; but I was with a particular dire girl and we were treading close to peripety.

Thus: if the Barbican and the NT green room are high culture, I can confirm that one was then complicitously on call to minor thespian royalty, not at all ripe for the edifyingly coarse dismissals in the refined epistles of Mr Pope.

47

If this is going to be your testament best press on with it. Trust that its true
    being is song.
Could anomalies in earth's magnetic field account for the inadequate overall
    yield of my similes?
Or is it that in a chance certain hour I read Aristotle on the mind's power
    to make disparates cohere: like the oxygen constituent of air, fuel that
    combusts into metaphor it does not kill, though eventually it will kill us.
To say this awkwardly or not at all.
The marginalizing of the aboriginal. The chant at the core of things marginal,
    something more than mere regional cant.
What is meant by 'original', if we mean much at all, other than to let fall our
    offerings into a pristine sacral well, a practice found appealing by some
    who think of the poem as faith-healing, a claim on the spirit that faith-
    healers inherit and have by heart?
More like that, I now feel, than the symbol I stole from unread Stendhal to
    garnish a mood: the crystalline saline bough and its wondrous frozen
    show that I took to be style before the spell broke and scattered filigree
    like spruce-ice in Calgary (a simile for luck).
Is it that predatory wealth attaches to history as if it were an arbitrary stealth
    of nature?
That we are employed as human shields in overriding force-fields by those
    who guide them towards the untenable sanctities of abiding things, our
    so-called citadels of words?

48

A sizeable sway-spread of mallow, familiar its mauve colour in the garden cove:
    a fine-brushed bluish tint that is there somewhere, almost too faint to
    call, perhaps a light-trick transference from the blue rose brick wall; and
    with a first blurring transparency of new rain in the air.
Desire to have things merely be as they are. To say nothing. Insidiousness of
    metaphor; perception not set free with its remarkable power to see; the
    unreachable itch in the brain to snatch metaphysical spoil for gain.
The lure of conclusion with no notion where to begin.

49

In the City the Wren spires seem infinitely variable in the logometrics of time,
  spiritually intrinsic, the patterns of quickened stone acclaiming suitably,
  as in a children's rhyme or the one hundred and fiftieth psalm.
But whatever it is they do towards God's glory they do not know it, as Hopkins
  more or less said, that admirably level-headed and objective poet.

50

Wanted: poet with small boat skills, reasonably well-haunted; imagination
  varied but without frills.
The secret sick heart is greedy for parody that is quick to reroot.
England's varying margins and hinterlands revealed in the strange heritage
  of the detective story: men with damp moustaches and carbide lamps
  combing the Essex marshes at low tide.
Avoid the antiques trade, the semiotic shifts between jet and jade.
Let us treat with sobriety the sober piety of the City financiers.
The beauty of the restored Wren churches should be a matter of record,
  indeed of gratitude; or, failing that, of duty.

51

Look up 'Fury' in the sane *Dictionary*; get her with torch and trimmings, the
  entire scenario of ancient and modern namings. Look up 'fiduciary'.
  What is a 'fiduciary symbol' to make us tremble?
Or, to invoke the archaic metaphor *Terribilità*: to find a new anarchy bearable
  because irreparable, as with a declaration of war?
Croesus embraces Midas—the heart of that unparticular vortex is motionless.
No tremor touches the City churches though for a moment they appear
  transparent.
The unimaginable power of the neutron adheres to imagination but does not
  sustain an image. There is absolutely no damage but we are gone.

52

Rigorously esteemed Gill for whom hair-cloth might be deemed wearable, if
    not bearable; his stone parable *Christ driving the money-changers from the*
    Temple rightly judged admirable, a congruent masterpiece re corporate
    usury, a matter on which he could be trusted to be sound: Ruskin,
    Morris, Belloc, Chesterton, made to do three-dimensional service, cari-
    tas in the round; plus, I confess, that slightly suspect reverence for the
    well-scrubbed-latrine-like simplicity of Dominican rule: that same Gill
    who, in some protracted fit of hiatus, abused his own daughters. When
    we enter the domain of guilt and complicity we enter a slaughterhouse.

53

From Battle of Britain to Festival of Britain was no big hop. In both a pleasant
    natural landscape gave cause for hope, faith even; despite an overriding
    impression of good breeding under strain.
Smoke rising in continual ravel; the Pool of London unpausing.
Like a fighter pilot in peacetime, part of a Meteor speed record-breaking team,
    I try not to portray hubris as I crack nonchalantly a block of Cadbury's,
    applying thumb and first finger pressures.
Or I am nullifying the danger of an unexploded bomb, re-opening the old
    fissures, again with that Cadbury's packet in my discarded greatcoat
    pocket; narrowly manipulative, scared; far from dumb though well
    prepared by our national tradition to look it.
When the Dutch, off the mouth of the Medway, were trading shot with our
    fleet, Dryden, out on the tideway in a small boat, was making headway
    with some members of the élite. They were amusing their ears with the
    future of theatre while about them the airs were gently concussing.
Good behaviour under strain, however, is not always the *vade mecum* to a
    Grade A epic poem. Its provenance, its credence, may be a madman's
    bad riddance in Bedlam.
Who stood as legal assignee of *Jubilate Agno* I cannot say.

54

A Cardington airship shed is grand once you comprehend its purpose of monstrous birthing and repose.

But Cardington is not Coventry whatever appearance maintains contrary.

The cathedral's curse is to have to endorse the misinvited sacred Muse; Sutherland's ill-favoured Creator presiding over a universe of subservient matter, seemingly intended for the investiture of Sepp Blatter and his spiritual kindred.

55

In Israel poets drive tanks; not because poets deserve to or thrive so; some have to, for the state to survive.

Israel has drunk eisel but let evil run; though it may not have meant to, even as it began to.

The world's mass is a mess of schism. Inside the gross a flawless prism of distress.

Creativity a contagious disease, as is romantic nationalism.

Name your (notional) ambition at three score and twice ten, then?

To be laic, sub-literary Latin Secretary to the nation, despite the archaic nature of fame and metaphor and things in that way heroic.

If truth's told, to flake out while punning that, at worst, is like panning for lost gold.

56

Again I use quasi-telegraphese to deliver the ever-importunate Muse.

'At the end of the day' opportunity and importunity hold sway.

Shock diamonds vibrate in the afterburners of her incessant demands.

She eats slow learners and farts them away.

57

Gandhi's sleek adobe palazzo, which I recall having seen, a millionaire's child's
    playpen, so at odds with that small gaunt naked man, no matter how well
    he would fit in:

Go on, say, there is always a different agenda from the one we imagined.

Not even our law's Mercator, the *Institutes* his straight-lined equator, gives
    more than a grand hint of the eldorados of entitlement beyond Antarctica
    awaiting settlement.

In the acquiring of craft discipline, jazz is just fine.

Please, not to debate the fateful life of Mr Pope, as though it were, in its
    entirety, a masturbatory hate story; grotesque in his grotto, a tubercular
    aged putto.

58

The world keyed by plastic is gnostic. I, being old, can remember when it was
    merely a thick-skinned ember so I am told.

When last I visited the angelologies of southern Spain and Iran, my small black
    and white screen turned all as spectral as the Shroud of Turin which is
    itself gnostic like the *duende*.

Plastic gnosis more resembles a mass psychosis. *Duende* does not, being a mat-
    ter of the pristine note possessing the singer's throat like a stoat in a
    warren; at once ripe and barren, a glut of sparse sorrow. I could go on,
    treading the same spot, old, undiminished, until late tomorrow; still not
    have finished.

59

By gnosis I mean both what it ought to have been and what it is, to tell truth.

O it is an all youth! is a true gnosis: the body at first no obstacle to the erotic
    soul but its oracle.

True gnosis is moved by self-loss to redeemed stasis. False gnosis never
    changes but in its agents, and is demeaned.

Widely applauded honours and prizes are false gnosis. So is 'the World
    rejoices'.

As for cost: refuse to be drawn on—by mere euphony, I suggest—to suppose
    our loves remain.

60

Michael and Gabriel sit in transparent regalia; as things were in Eden before
the first midden, before the first falling of male hair, even before you and
I strayed briefly there.

Esaddaeus rightly or wrongly I think of as more like us, though free from
divinely-transmitted disease and the worst of our plebeian proclivities.

Baruch is third of the twelve paternal angels. Seven are missing, removed
either by mischance or by some right gem of mischoosing.

Hard to tell how far original Eden was fed by photosynthesis if at all, or
whether so-called gnostics drew therefrom a form of proto-sin-thesis,
self-breeding syncretic loves denuding the apple trees in prevailing droves.

Painters such as Cranach seem to have grasped the psychopathology of the
Fall pretty well. Desire is asped: it is the theology of 'once bitten', temp-
tation's consequence up to our self-willed ictus: the image does not
entirely correct us.

Mutual forlornness can be beautiful; though those locked desirous eyes are hell.

61

Is it the blood-infused chalk that has raised an outcry ('*sous la craie blanche qui
criait*'), or ('*le sang invisible*') the blood itself?

Once again, Frénaud, ever unmet-with old fatal friend, I have ripped you off
in our potter's field of intellectual property by attempting to translate
you blind.

The aporia is a-porose whereas chalk is porous.

Metabolism is an embolism at our age; not a shot of jism.

Aural symmetry maybe attainable; moral chemistry in chaos.

The never-virgin chalk, so susceptible to penetration.

I am making a trim symbolism of the Somme, which is what it will have become
by the time we are through with the next four years of profitable tears.

You were a prisoner in *la deuxième guerre*; and morose about it. I should have
thought you had every right.

Les Rois Mages, a slow processional through France's Herodian plight, was
true to both voices, yours and hers, but not in our tacky sense of the
word 'confessional'. With that out of the way, it can be termed a confes-
sion if one so chooses, as is true of most more than half-decent poetry;
and has its uses.

62

Why such irony in re the mystical context when a graph of even the most commonplace exchange would appear perplexed; when we drop out from the plainest statement in the posture of a bat?

So, decide to make something of that, the style to resemble an English *Aeneid* or *Iliad*. Do it like Dryden. No, up the bid. Do it as Wren did it at the Sheldonian, which is like Dryden in stone.

You've always been a name-dropper.

I believe I need them to charm away scrofula such as Sam Johnson suffered from. 'Chronic enlargement and degeneration of the lymphatic glands.' Thought to be healed by the application of regal well-anointed hands. Dryden and Wren are kings; and English poetry has lately incurred something squatly debilitating to the strength of even the most common word.

There you go again: it's as if you inject fame-serum to sustain self-harm.

Earth clodding sky, boding to bring down, embattled aurochs. Now a notched knurl of bone, six thousand years on, where its remains were interred with some rite or were simply thrown.

63

Puff that butterfly encomium from the palm of your hand, and there will be rain in Australia, the first in years; and fruit of your creative powers plus your editor's.

We are in a continuum which is entitlement by another name: inter-emblematic sparrows and the like; and not one fretted wingtip in the air merely as a unique freak-trip.

'No child born to die', so they say.

Postmortem political diaries perform their curious, coarsely-finessed game: fealty, lealty, arousal, espousal, betrayal, blame.

Minor Restoration drama of Thatcherism's high old time at the Tote.

'No child born to die' is pitiful in a different category of common folly.

64

Cringingly presumptuous, spiderishly grandiose, barbarously otiose, Britannia in her woes.

I wish I didn't think that. I am an old-fashioned patriot even though, long ago, I fell to praising the Easter Rising.

Our fellow citizens, chiefly, make fools of us; not uncommonly at grand funerals and the unveiling of national memorials.

Nelson, pickled in rum, or brandy, as some claim, on the voyage home, now with Wolsey's sarcophagus for a tomb: opulence and opportunism, under Paul's dome where—I repeat—you expect the lightest footfall to go boom.

There are fools enough to be made fools of, I grant you that.

Romantic nationalism (*supra*) is a kind of fate.

65

Hammerklavier hammering the middle ear, a music quiz clue on cultural radio: drum, anvil, hammer, in quasi-musical clamour; the brimming chamber pot; the wires of the Broadwood pranged out. The heavens mute; grandeur as something brute; genius as primogeniture in the gens.

Genius cannot comprehend its own ens; at times not to be distinguished with strongest lens; yet strong enough to barrack its own song, it is the most abiding of things lost.

Dunce that I am; even so, hooked on Pope's demo in the *Dunciad Variorum*; dulness spooked and sparked into infinite variety of *drôles-de-drame* within the genius-struck donkey work of rhyme; anarchy booked; honesty at premium.

66

(Of Stauffenberg—his schrecked luck—it is best not to try to speak.)

Antony's death was in truth messy and lingering. He botched it, like General
    Beck at the Bendlerstrasse that eventful evening in July.

I could not have watched it; nor could you. Legend does not like us; unlike
    Eros we do not know what to do.

But look again at the matter: though Eros was quick he was a selfish prick,
    ditching Antony who deserved better and who is to be commended for
    his instinctive courtesy—giving Eros credit for the neat way he did it—
    having been stranded like a self-duped whale under a sea-wall.

Yes, Antony comes out of it well, biting on pain and with an embowelled smell.

67

Take up the self-draining pen: a slow clatter-dither of ancient machinery
    getting it together again.

All gnostics know that steam power was temperamental and probably pos-
    sessed a soul; at unpredictable times could fly off the handle and cause
    screams. The 'permanent way' was entirely as Turner sensed it—
    something holy—who brought all to display. It truly did shimmer on
    heat like that. Shakespeare would have wrought wonders with steam in
    A Midsummer Night's Dream.

Why—strangely—does something wondrous not now stoop from an ancient
    Greek tragic metaphor, to which reason angrily surrenders its logical,
    pseudo-legal power; and dictate, albeit with mute stare, what is always
    and undeniably there; and will be seen to have been so, where now only
    posthumous mute justice ill-advisedly, warily, sets a toe?

The soul in its form knows where it is from.

68

O, the Tower, O, the towering edifices of high finance, where old solid money
    becomes ferocity's cladding in zigzag patterns glazed like faience.

Say that we meet—even now it pays to be discreet—for an echoic stroll along
    Black Friar's Lane by Apothecaries' Hall; ice-sculptures marking the
    vital impermanence of things sacral.

My heart a little sore—the pacemaker-size virtual reality projector unexpect-
    edly tricky to instal—but all's well; though, is it advisable, if we get as far
    as that thoroughfare, to take the elevated walkway along London Wall?
    A thrill, would it be, to encounter a still centurion of stone?

Briskly the dark displays mimes of tame risk, with sherbet fountains and Very
    lights innocent of maintenance.

When you say 'old solid money', what exactly do you mean?

I suppose that at heart I mean intrinsic value coin, such as the cartwheel tup-
    pence of seventeen ninety-seven: not fit for purpose—folk would need
    sacks for purses; and the price of copper was of course variable. Too big,
    too heavy, for a small child's hand; therefore a grand gift encouraging
    thrift. You could make it trundle-wobble on a deal table. Together with a
    raggety peg-doll something in a child's special dimension real.

I am happy to explain what I feel and why.

That which cheapens is no part of real economy.

Speculative money set hatching is like coney-catching.

Piers Plowman Histories, as I recall, we read at school, though I do not remem-
    ber if we did John Ball whom the royal butchers set-to with a will to
    dismember.

Still here, old dear, admirable lay-figure that you are?

Usury is not wholly unlike perjury, I sense; or some manner of injury sans
    recompense.

Why are we so defeated, so dense, year after year, only to disappear; and why
    the dire permanence of pretence?

69

The way the lime leaves darken in high summer; then it begins to blow and low
    rainclouds come churning across and the sun takes his chamber: I love
    this atmosphere-laden afternoon as I do Tennyson.

Intelligence matters. Even *In Memoriam* is an emotional scam drawn on
    the pieties of our social betters, including high-collared men of science
    and letters.

There is a strong lyric charge in each song from *The Princess*. What I miss is
    some obduracy of the mind's address which Péguy has and in which he
    is at one with the imperturbable Beauce.

The most fragile things, like wing pollen on a daymoth's wings, are true to,
    and at one with, the measurings of cosmic survival; outside, that is, the
    haloes of black holes.

70

Almost always the wrong people are admired, rewarded, and sedulously
    guarded; it is how things are wired and starred.

Intrinsic value falls vacant if it is vacantly hoarded. It needs to make account to
    its own counterpoint, as in *Death and the Maiden*.

Schubert in those quartets writes well for the cello; gives it a lot to do; in the
    Quintet strenuously engages with two.

Having created that, could you tacitly consent to become simply a declension
    of fate? To be so bidden, having been so self-ridden?

To be shut down like a reactor because of the stress factor.

To have the security light come on long after you have gone; to be declared an
    inexplicable phenomenon, a benign anon.

To have light eternal, eternal rest, thrust upon you like an unsolicited call;
    unsolicited but not random.

And yet genius itself is out of series; and is aroused by strange nocturnal voices
    of St Lucy's day that are not refused.

As the amber bristles with its brushed electrons—remember?—even though,
    or because, the etymology is so dodgy.

Have the dodginess on the house. It is the least of my worries. It goes with the
    dithyramb.

71

A working poem has, or is, its own microclimate; certainly, in Britain it does so
    possess its nous. Some of us may be distinguished thus, pre-structuralists
    of our antic cause; the streamlet's cluck and treble through meadow and
    arable; gold gobs of mistletoe, the spoiler, the spoils, heaped in Tenbury
    market to go.
Something here to be garbled if part understood. I am invoking presence not
    mood. Mood—almost at first standing—abandons us while, in absence,
    presence remains. I state it crudely enough for small gains.
But it is not, even so, the same as the 'strain of time' which, according to that
    Jesuit (resolute, glad, forlorn), draws from us the psychic skin that bound
    us to find the world tolerable, ourselves credible; and reels it in: alien
    earth a photonegative of all earthly loves; the Aurora palpitating absently
    apart in its waves and coils.
How, knowing this, he could write 'Hurrahing in Harvest' I can barely
    conceive; though it reflects and reveals 'Spelt from Sibyl's Leaves',
    mutely audible, darkly lucent, impenetrable, starkly provident.

72

Luck, past a certain stage, strikes me as automatic, and can unstick old age.
The mingled throps and thrangs of bell-ropes and bell metal, mangled and
    muffled songs, when you stand beneath the bell chamber, hearing the
    ropes grunt and clamber.
And you think visceral, you think hardly at all:
Could cough up the phlegm of a poem but only if you are some good.

73

My brain (he yet again confides) is St Bride's tower, bell-confused while the
    bells take plunging fatal rides inside an hour.
Or say, a Ländler-type funeral prance let rip for Mahlerians.
'To run on empty is to achieve a sort of hallucinatory abundance and clarity.'
In truth he is a Parnassian and a sassy man.

74

Tumbledown Dick was got rid of with an easygoing kick.

A total loser, yet he was spared the regicides' *via dolorosa*, the theatre of power that London must attend in fear and joyful hysteria, ready for a bloody eyeful.

Tyburn, Charing Cross: a man of servile class rips hearts from torsos. Mystic neo-statists give voice, declaring it is like shovelling refuse from a lately forsaken, trashed, fiercely repossessed house.

Why do we ever doubt the efficacy of quick-witted grovelling, of double dealing, of bare-faced malevolence that stares us out, shedding the last sham courtesy of pretence?

With Tumbledown Dick we seem part way to Addison's half-civil Town, or to the Languishes of Worcestershire, to the 'Country Wife', to sensibility and the waywardly contented, sadly hopeful life; the woodshed, imbrued chopping-board, the outrageous parrot's favourite tirade or riff.

75

As, many times, motive is inaccessible, must we get used to the art of the plausible, and let live? And thrive as prats do on chat shows, toasting each other in bat juice, and coasting?

I would not encourage others of my late age to be always handling a proximity-fuse of indignant rage to demonstrate the art of self-harming. Keep counsel, stay charming, I now advise.

Politics and law back then—Age of Milton, I mean—were visceral; poetry not; though republicans read the *Pharsalia*, inter alia, and imitated it a lot. To Lucan, indeed, 'viscera' was a word forty and more times taken up, buzzing the era.

Coriolanus worked best by being intravenous; no great effusion of plaudits, then, for that particular manifest. It could entertain, sustain, its meaning by means subterrane. It came to the surface, for instance, in Paris in the nineteen thirties rendering each clangorous scene timely and dangerous.

Great poetry is visceral now; felt so, at any rate, by the deeply read: a living power bearing back, I believe, some notice of us to the still-witnessing dead.

The radical incompatibility of those spiritually able. Why?

76

After the Armistice many who were stricken in mind became chicken farmers.
    Check this out if you like. Check Larkin?
The turning undead-returning world pivoted on a meshed, barren and
    curd-pashed field.
English Journey, *Sagittarius Rising*, the Thiepval Memorial to the Missing of the
    Somme: these three for my money, any time, though they do not rhyme.
I don't remember chicken farm as a Larkin theme. Are you thinking of
    'Wedding Wind'?
We could agree that a (good) poem is a way of staking a claim to the esteem
    which by custom attaches to land: *Coke upon Littleton* again, plus 'Legal
    Fiction', and indeed Empson's diction *passim*.
'Himmler was a chicken farmer. It's in my thesis with an ethical disclaimer.'
A great poet who fixates on landed estates is of course Yeats.
For Dryden, Castle Ashby, possibly, was his never-possessed—but therefore
    never lost?—Eden.
One could, I imagine, press on to success in this vein: of poetry's being
    deprivation's gain; of Captain Douglas's failed 'twenties chicken farm;
    and of *Alamein to Zem Zem*.

77

The 'Irish Salamis': a commonplace flourish (Yeats) about the clerkly author
    of *Tar Water* (Berkeley).
He was sending intelligence out for audition; he believed a win would be good
    for the nation, the mind of Ireland freed, raw body, old head, albeit
    Swift died mad.
The 'Irish Salamis' is a price you must pay for some victory over and above
    Pearse and Connolly and the 'right rose tree'. It is, as he said, also 'liable
    to bias'.
The Queen at the wall in Ireland was not entirely unlike Willy Brandt at the
    Ghetto memorial.
Whether 'the ultimate reality must be anarchy' who can presume to say?
'Tradition is kindred': perhaps that is true; perhaps a great cross-roaded mind
    has blundered: 'nadir to nadir', riches to rags; in the temple of order
    decapitated stone figures struck from niches; mobbed cattle with their
    drool and ordure; at their hooves dogs.

78

'A flood, a comet, or a monstrous birth, send a thrill throughout England', our
    grand old sing-along land.

Less often, these days, time-spawned by antique blood or ancient worth of
    abode, which ought to be to the good.

And yet—quaint shame missing from frame—absentee banditry more than
    ever usurps the time; buy-to-rent tenement, to apartment, to penthouse.

Choose best whom you most wish to be. The grammar is solipsistic.

Do not spladge that name with lipstick on a mirror, so that you must cancel it
    in terror with shaving foam.

Creativity as a ward in Medicine City I can accept—many are raving—but not
    as a piece of spiritual equity. Nor as another name for introverted ritual
    behaving; nor even as ungifted honest striving.

Douglas, the 'reactionary horseman' of Merton, could have 'done' Marston
    Moor as he 'did' post-Alamein in pen and watercolour; a bit like a
    cartoon.

Major Player, the cigarette millionaire, was his superior at the war.

Were they once, tee-hee, anti-Luddite, anti-Chartist, Nottinghamshire
    yeomanry?

Douglas was much more. If that is ambiguous I'm sorry.

History is not mere chronicles plus competing doctorals.

Crapaud (OED) is the large jewel grown by tautological accrual in the slow
    forehead of a toad.

79

Be as good as the *Sun* once was with a headline pun. Learn skills wherever you
    can and don't brood on your ills, is my attitude.

'Poets make things up', for example, sounds simple but was a terrific scoop.

Handel supporting the Witch of Endor with multi-bassoon grandeur in
    Saul is a reminder to us all of how profound the accessible can be,
    given mastery.

I feed these words to my mouth and gut like bismuth, but without allaying the
    complex pains of such need. Know what I'm saying?

Was it indeed Rebus's dad who asked, as a kind of test, 'to write a good poem
    is it best to be in a dwam'?

There is a tipping-point where the constraint of gravity yields to momentum
    in both centrum and rim, all in a moment; this is the commencement
    of a poem: sheer energy without any display; mere synergy, where *mere*
    means *entire*.

Recently I have heard it said, of a single steam-driven driving wheel off the
    axle, manhandled for routine overhaul: *momentum is your friend.*

I do not want this to end but it will; be both transient and still.

80

If Radio Three is kept on continuous play you hear from time to time some
    extraordinary theme.

Eventually things come in at the ears that come out of the eyes as tears.

Integrity is textual above all, though what my motive is for claiming this you
    will perceive.

81

Repeat: what I love and admire is true gnosis; everything that I hate is not. Stated so, it is rough but adequate; sufficient to get the right things done, I mean. Of my thesis this is the ghost-score.

Vanbrugh (yet again): slightly top-heavy *sprezzatura* man, premeditatedly without plan. I find myself drawn into his radius and span, although my own pair of dividers has a warped spine.

No-one now will shout, 'he cribbed that from Donne, the old goat'. Critical mass they are not.

Leave me a wordless message of note on my cordless poem. Why for a moment consider anything more or less remote at this time, other than your name?

The rattle-voiced war-'special' does unrattled performances in his officious spot half-way along the landlord-walloped and cracked street.

I cannot yet hear the odd off-beat of Benz and Jumo engines.

True gnosis is obsessed with small alien details of fact.

What I call 'false gnosis' is not mere hypothesis: far from it; but uses false deduction and induction, such as 'sleep tight!'

82

Ah, yes, the black and white war-goddess, Jumo: she so loves to strum and rhyme and begin on time.

She is a compelling figure, her echelons of swagger, the aviators her avatars; like them she wears trim duelling-scars.

Definitely a bad gnosis; and a bad prognosis for London in nineteen forty and forty-one: those virginal Wren churches—now you see them, now they are gone. Jumo is a weighty conjurer.

What stood central remains ill-befallen and marginal because of her.

After ten years a thin inconstant curtain of rain will drape the Festival of Britain across a nude cityscape that by then does not appear odd.

83

When I praise Douglas and Allison I mourn more than a couple of gifted men
who died too soon.

They confronted the language with which few engage or contend; saw it as
neither quite enemy nor quite friend.

The 'creative spirit' is of no more use or merit than skiddy or tacky blood in
the guts of a wrecked tank, or a gutted body, if words are an unrecipro-
cating blank, a putty-impress of vague pity, a caption-block aswarm with
balm-intoxicated flies, an unrelieved irritant, merely, of more distress.

This insight, this gift of a sort, they rewrought and left in mid-stride, if only
as their punitively celibate yet bereft bride.

84

Robert Falcon Scott was a true mystic of muddle-through; and, like his crew,
appealed to old RVW, he of the Agnostic rite, who chipped and snow-
blasted a symphony from the grimly sentimental plot and the inclusive-
exclusive, active-passive, of Scott's valedictory note.

I'm glad the old man got himself together again later and delivered the Ninth
before his transmigration from podium to plinth.

If Scott had not died when he did, Jutland could have been his lot: one of
Jackie Fisher's divas, the inadequately armoured new battle cruisers,
would have taken him with her, and eight or nine hundred other heroes,
bruisers, losers, and skivers.

85

Fisher and RVW were brothers-in-law. Hegemony had—still has—cultural
hierarchy, even intrinsic value, in tow.

It's a mystery, as they proclaim in that jolly sad Shakespeare film.

There's old Jackie fuming at the helm.

There's RVW, volunteering even though over-age. God bless the pastoral
realm of our good dream and present rage.

Here I am, my pate always well below the parapet, skulking with you, brother
sub-Average for whom I do not rightly care; and with you, cousin Nym.

I bless the marvellous 'Five Mystical Songs': although strong music cannot
even begin to mend wrongs, it is, in some way I wish I could well relate,
analogous to the Pentecostal tongues.

86

'Fastidious fumes' and 'melancholick blood' make you inclined to brood. Not
     to speak of rheums, my old dove of the tombs. Don't leave.

'Poussaient des cris de joie'? Not he, not she; not we.

'Job, an old and humbled man', sits right foot forward with his detraumatized
     wife in their recovered, re-revered life, both blessing the large-print
     liner notes, edited records of repetitious but instructive grief.

87

The rattlesnake can track its own venom; it injects its prey, letting it briefly run
     then drop and die. The snake follows through in its course to consume.

Poems that have you feel 'how true' are variable forms of *trompe-l'œil*.

A myriad delicate sense-membranes may fail to home on, hunt down, the
     Muse in as many lines of badly-presumptive verse.

'Poets make things up' will always remain the occasion of our profession,
     I hope.

88

'Anhedral', 'dihedral', terms of true gnosis in *Aircraft Recognition* of nineteen
     forty-one, that now happily famous time of crisis.

'Recognition mnemonics' I took as testamentary to witness, though I had no
     Greek. I may have thought Mnem a pharaoh: that bit I'm not sure about.

'Mnemon', now so rounded, nubile and sleek, was yet unborn; nothing that
     I then knew of could threaten my tiny prepubertal thorn.

Salvation is so apart from oneself it could be the golden calf.

The trim black Dornier, intent on attack, hung aloof and near, turning into its
     run for the Longbridge Austin: a plane that had been drawn by a first-
     rate child artist, in three dimensions.

It might even be real; there was a sound both shrill and profound, unheard;
     felt, rather, with the skin; and felt so again when I sensed for the first
     time the sex of a girl.

A Dornier's 'uniformly tapered wings', for seventy years high in my gnostic
     categories of divine things.

89

'The scent-antennae of the tobacco hawk moth seek out the classical honey of
the poet's mouth.'

Orphée claimed Résistance credentials by such windfalls. He was taken at his
word: the codes from London were always that absurd.

Nitrogen creates rare blue jets in tempestuous upper air.

Surrealism had presumptions to schism: it is an effort not to dislike them and
their high old Parisian time.

As ever I exempt Desnos, enter him under *good gnosis*, his deep, sad feline jokes
and serious, who, starved of penicillin, was served piecemeal to death
by lice.

90

Baruch, I've said, is third of the twelve paternal angels. I hope to approach him
from a variety of angles like the tall theorems striding erect in their
divine pact through the schoolrooms.

In the kind of lycée that Péguy and Rimbaud attended, Euclid and Virgil
amicably bonded, Pythagoras stalked the halls and no-one minded.

Rouault's *Miserere* for some reason was to be prize book of the session. Work
began at the edge of the Great Grimpen War, and ended, after ten years
and more, in the cage of carnal roar when Paris appeared to some as the
Great Whore (others cast Weimar as the brazen screamer).

Rouault was in effect right to oppose absolute black to absolute white while
permitting weak intercessions of greyish half-tone into the machinations
of the block.

Péguy I still acclaim as the greatest near-anonym of that time. He both appor-
tioned and bore blame crucially; unlike Cocteau with his fey *poésie* and
naughty opium; and apart from Rouault's mystical aggressive passivity.

Compared to all such *The Book of Baruch* is easy going, compliant with my
disproportionate ideal, surviving surreal mismanagement with humour
and style; collapsible for ease of stowing.

91

Wanting a right reason to contain wrath-on-the-brain, if only in this late
season before night and death, I have to conclude that it is a legitimate
brood and foison and may create things of worth.

Catullus and Sextus Propertius I have never known all that well and, of
course, I found Propertius in Pound. I take a pull on these names as a
sexton would have hauled on a passing bell in former times.

Cultural name-dropping is for me like taking a cut-price river-cruise wherein
I revisit many a pleasure house of self-abuse, without undue moping or
over-stopping.

I cannot see what you might say to me that would be treatable as good advice.

It was different when, though even then too late, you taught Desnos how to
treat lice.

Desnos was predestined to pick gnosis and to speak vatically without hypnosis
which—this is a refrain!—was not my scene then.

I now plan to call on alchemical Nicolas Flamel, the public notary, at his *siège*
under the Tour St-Jacques, and ask him to re-edify my rage.

Desnos, who could tell a spell from a fake, kicked about like a foal in an oratory,
for sheer unsullied joy, and not an item fell into disarray.

There is much dry satisfaction in the obscene; but after that you need seriously
to retune; something I have never yet contrived to get done.

Hear this: 'I fear to die like Arius in a boghouse made notorious by my demise'.

92

The original poem, according to strong rumour, was a boomerang. Or an
alarm-pheromone. Sound evidence there is none.

Neo-patristic exegeses have bred Dan Brown-type cénacles like ripe cheeses;
not dissimilar to the madhouse in act four of *Peer Gynt* or the overall
tenor of *No More Parades*.

The great have, all without exception, done their stint among the shades.

Found himself not to be dead; and had to administer roll-call, after having
gone over the top numbly, without hope.

There should be a rule, a judgement, a justice, of silence; but that's not prac-
ticable when you've so heartily backed your own oratory, constructed a
fable well worthy of the Nobel.

The tills of commemoration blart and sing, all short-changing the ills of the
nation.

93

Constipation, some say and I may agree, sat at the root of the Arian heresy.

They claim a similar thing, but on stronger evidence, for Luther among the Augustinians.

Coleridge was in dire straits on the voyage to Malta; squatted for hours over basins of boiling water.

Waugh died of a heart attack, endeavouring to process his cack.

More of the great have died thus than have been brought to choke on hemlock, I choose to suppose.

The elect hierarchies of paradise have swung around the rigid status of our dung.

94

This word 'great' that I leave about like a tip under a plate or like a *carte de visite*?

The great, let me repeat, are the dead of whom I approve, whom indeed I love.

I have this need to anticipate objections from the few who can still read: though few, yet many factions.

'Lord, how the world makes nothing of the memory of a man!'

Here I am, stuck with that proposal; and none who might fake wise counsel or even move me to mild sexual arousal.

I cannot let the pity of it go; nor can I forget Eliot, 'the dead are what we know', though I've had to tweak that a bit.

Words attract words as trouble attracts trouble and yet, to succeed, we must ditch all safeguards; and see and think and speak double.

95

For the most part I forget—it seems not to fit—Yeats's debt to France, and
  how he could incorporate that with the dance of the intellect, or
  intelligence.

The Green Helmet, nineteen ten, carries an erratum slip tipped into page one
  confessing that on pages one to six—poems of dream-wedded idealized
  sex—he wrote 'Raymond Lully' in error for 'Nicolas Flamel'.

'No Second Troy' needs no apology.

So that, in re-reading Desnos on the alchemical, I sense something slender but
  continuous and intense that I can render of use to my own verse: this
  I am eager to confess, though the issue, the residue, is so meagre.

Flamel and alchemy, for Yeats, were Eros and Maud Gonne and a love that had
  become flame in a stone.

Per Amica Silentia Lunae, of nineteen seventeen, plays a hidden variant of
  the tune; for here Yeats is guilty of breach of fealty. It is Iseult, Maud
  Gonne's daughter, who is subject—or object—of his cult.

Something famous and heroic in a major key, by Charles Péguy, Iseult had read
  to him; and some Francis Jammes; and poems by one or two other
  names; and a poem by Jammes 'made us cry'.

Ah, sex and poetry! A double luxury of power and loss. And, after more than a
  century, who cares a toss, apart from an empowered scholar busy at her
  biographical-critical double entry? And they are gone, the rebellious
  foiled hearts and the old gentry.

'Per amica silentia lunae'—the phrase—did not at all mean what it says or
  appears to say: the allusion is to a radical treachery and to popular mass
  delusion creating a dire lesion in the civic wall. It clocks-in to Troy's
  adulterate fall, aptly enough given those secret and mass hysterias;
  ignores the remnant virility recouping in Italy and—as legend holds
  sway—in Gross Britannia.

Surely a bit too early, some may reply: there would be thrumming and obscene
  drumming soon, and 'The Second Coming'.

96

And, yes, I realize, and part of my mind does grasp, that a till, now, is near-noiseless on the odd occasions that we use coins. It's as easy as making a wish or issuing an all but mute sigh or gasp.

There has not been, for many a year, that brassy *clash-cling*; nor does a tele-phone now do *brr-brr* or *brrng-brrng*.

Things are not now, in the old sense, monetary; and this has reduced the odd beauty of some kinds of onomatopoeia; and makes me a collector of drab thick-copper coins and re-reader of *Little Grey Rabbit*; even though I do not, on seeing some stone-encased brass, automatically rub it; though I could not estimate the equivalent of a cubit. Do I unnecessarily repeat?

The very nature of the lyric is now archaic, though not like Nineveh and Tyre. Perhaps more like Torah and Talmud. At least one is released from the subjective brood and sham relevance of mood into the freedom of the inexorable semitic-semantic code.

But because I am not a Jew I desire to know all that was said when, once a year, the high priest convened in holy fear with the Ark of God.

David danced before the Ark, and the daughter of Saul made a mock and was struck barren.

And Uzzah put his hand out to save it when the cart wobbled, and fell dead upon stony ground.

Whereas David was barbarously ennobled.

Predestination and luck co-exist in hard-to-ride tandem; and the divinely choreographed many times performs as if it were random or stuck.

'The poet as Uzzah' is a temptation to make and break prophecy by deliberate misreading of what the text is in fact not hiding; and by a disregarding of imaginative tact.

97

It could have been a joy to possess the original Morse key in full working order
    as a learning toy:

An early edition of *Gray's Anatomy* to aid my dissection of difficult poetry:

Foxe's Book of Martyrs, my father's *Police Gazette*, Blake's *Job with his Sons
    and Daughters*, and I'd be all set:

I would launch down the greased slip with a screech of champagne, the
    red-gold grin not yet in place between my cold coal-fired lips.

I could name scores of enemy aircraft and dozens of Royal Navy ships.

The true genius of *Gray's Anatomy* was its illustrator, the ill-used and
    defrauded Carter.

It is a pity, all things considered, that I never grew up, although I can do anat-
    omies in my sleep.

98

Lubricious Chlamydia, patron saint of the media—

Heresy is gnosticism and the prosecution of heretics is a gnostic practice.

Moral essays were powerful ways of maintaining a quarrel, but not these days.

Learn from celebrity populism a form, a slattern charisma.

Economy does not rhyme with money and ennui but with anomie (I have
    blurred the paradigm; it is sentimentally absurd).

Dunce that I am I am nonetheless hooked on Pope's maleficent dream in the
    Dunciad Variorum.

99

I swipe myself again in my rawest spot, my logical dyslexia. I cannot shape up
    to formal reasoning any more than I can cope with the tax year.

But I have fee'd help with my taxes. As to this other, it must be some defi-
    ciency in cerebral texture. I am become approximate and, as I say too
    often, *hexed*.

I find this shaming; and slip into something comfortable, such as self-harming,
    when I am able.

The crassest form of self-harm, that I have long practised, is the poem.

On how a fact becomes a 'wandering adjective': the facts of my being are now
    the adjectives of this work.

Indeed I love formal logic; it is to me a spectacle of delight, though I could
    never do it.

I have to stay this low key; it would be a relief to contrive rapturously; but such
    it is to conceive of another life.

That grammar combines without flinching the 'absolutely discrepant' explains
    why poetry is invented, but not how.

100

The cosmos is an alchemist of star-compost.

Our cells are the posthumous largesse of red giants; of supernovae the weird
    beneficiaries or clients.

The universal constants are of attraction and repulsion but not of love, nor
    does the solar wind infuse itself with the breath of God. There is phase
    but not mood.

There will not be one last dire blast of forgiveness laying all things waste; nor
    even a spreading boredom of stars with their own stardom.

I feel the unstrung language of faith recoil slenderly to a spool tongue-balancing
    behind my teeth.

101

Foghorn Leghorn and Roadrunner are a particular kind of winner. While their winning is not gaining anything, neither can happy idiocy ever fail. All is back on track ready for the next reel, for your 'bit of a laugh' philosophe.

Rid us—somebody—God—of callous ignorant administrators, lords of public want, sinecurists of their own failures, bearers of no brunt, inimical to dissent.

....

Jutland was a tactical victory, a strategic defeat, for the German High Seas Fleet.

Fritz blew to bits three of our finest ships, made riddance (*Gott mit uns*) of many more British chaps than we made of his.

But he could not break our sea-blockade; never tried strength again with our shoddily-manoeuvred, ill-armoured marine; for which we too praised the Divine.

Ah, mysteries and armouries, the manifold blessings of reprise!

....

The supercilious inefficient administrator rose to new strength during the Great War, when to call power chaotic was judged to be unpatriotic.

You will say that I cite the naive irrational Pound, who was not a British national.

He also attributed what he termed 'mind-ersatz' to the officialdom of the United States. I can supply you with quotes.

It would be good to effect, sometime, a pact between high style and political tract, preferably in rhyme.

102

Need and obligation contribute a little to the theatrical chorus of tradition.

This is meant to make us feel for the noble austerities of rule at a time when everything is up for sale without benefit to the people. A little touch of Harry or Hal, the squaddies' pal, which became 'none else of name' at the burial when the king had his game sewn up, and immortal fame.

Hard to believe that Shakespeare wrote 'A little touch of Harry' without bile; but such was his style and he had to live.

He used 'Will' in the sonnets to imply some form of libidinous shame urging his proud uneasy self to take blame—at once fawning and knowing and petty lading and seeking quarry; though, unlike most takers of his ilk, he gave back to the silk doers and slackers of that time a superior glory.

The toad, some aver, does not have a forehead adequate to bear a grand jewel of state in the discovery of the true nation; merely a warp of skin between its eyes.

But I'd guess that she probably does; as she goes, as she slowly rocks on her axis, as if she had but lately crawled from shrunken seas.

We are, even now, too much of service to the lords of indolent praxis, insolent show.

103

The shellac discs that hissed, with a faint noise of frying, on the latest and best cabinet gramophones while Elgar lay dying, pressed upon a last thin membrane of sense with unrelenting coherence not unlike a new tone, hitherto untapped, of pain.

Tall and art-deco, fretworked in front, with a fill-in of linen behind and between the design, like the wife of a toff even at ff, they could inspire fear.

Winding them was like starting a car with a kick-back handle; enough for a three-minute spin to the Coasts of Coromandel.

From the run-down 'table model' of my youth, sound was a muffled bawling in a booth.

104

The earth swings round its star with a misleading air of stolid grandeur, notwithstanding the vapours in which it is veiled.

I was excused my period of military servitude. Glad then, I now feel shame. I missed out on the great *rite de passage* of my time.

I was not aware of the aria for the two armed men.

I do not mean *L'homme armé* of Cabezón and others, nor any folk ballad of ill-fated twin brothers and fatal choices. Not the Beverley Sisters and their Christmas *Ohrwurm* taking our grim festivities to show by snowstorm.

If I went back, and then back, I might get something like *Old Moore's Almanack* or *The Magic Flute*.

I am as much of the folk as some cynosure of hale Northumbrian stock, some balladeer cupping his ear in the style that is *de rigueur* but which urges me to mock.

The tanks are grinding again at El Alamein, part now, not then, of time's grubbed attrition and trashbin; that Keith Douglas, the good soldier, is about to elect his eminent domain.

105

The poem begins as a small tight maelstrom somewhat at knee-height, not quite touching your shins.

Seriously? Seriously.

It gathers up and hosts briefly a variety of scrap. Variety is a misnomer but I am addressing the laity which chiefly desires escape via good humour.

Voracious the Muse of Redress in her eccentric shoes and tipsy corona of Christmas tree silver wire; though on Twelfth Night she goes out like a light.

Some form of theatrical decorum is essential to the asymmetrically radiant poem. Even Burns has his oblique theatre which includes tough carica- ture; though the mass sentimentalist does not concur, dreams him a drammed-up heart and a soul repining.

The secret of the thing—I repeat—is codified by the unnamed armed duo in *The Magic Flute* who negotiate their sentinel track through the estate of the late Bach whom many, then, would have thought beyond reach of the polite.

Mendelssohn in his fame championed him. Mozart did the same, but earlier. It would be strange to think this peculiar.

Some find my attitude alien, indeed rude, like something by Pasolini, like being nude, if you take my meaning.

The Ashes of Gramsci: I can find no legitimate rhyme for that last name lying about the rusting back-lot frame.

106

Stanley Spencer is yet another necromancer of familiar air: a spiritual-carnal marriage-mystic, which is a characteristic of others I'm disposed to admire. *The Chamber-Idyll* is dangerously chaste stuff; and in a sense Spencer calls its bluff. I would not have wished to encounter Miss Preece in the buff, perhaps because I'm a sexual poetaster.

The Marriage at Cana is also a form of resurrection, from which sexual inter- action is not set apart. Here, the groom maladroitly resets a chair; the bride smoothes the dress under her bum as she sits down. And, in their members, you and I can rebecome what we so briefly were, without mutual blame, without that wear-and-tear—

'Light sleep, second sweet bedfellow of the wedding night, do thou also confer, Hymen, breaker of hymens!'

With them in grief let us briefly identify before we go hence.

107

A sound there must have been, a millipede patter; it is one I no longer hear
    clearly through time's blur.
A tide-race of young frogs migrating, an exodus, for ten minutes or thereabouts:
Pond, back road, moist air; and these in their swift soft obduracy, this indivis-
    ible spasm of tenure:
The sun's ghosting through mist fans ectoplasm to flame.

108

Oddly that low tactic of Leda and the Swan is one to which *The Book of Baruch
    by the Gnostic Justin*, nothing if not eclectic, can be shown to allude.
'The sixth of the maternal angels was named Satan'—I don't see how the two
    mythic traditions could ever get on.
I intend to propose the Port Glasgow *Resurrection* as the true republic in its
    grandest realization, O thou who understandest.
As for the question whether erudition should be the foundation of the equitable
    state: if it were put to the vote I would affirm the noble fable.
If elected to the praesidium, unlike Senator Yeats I'd abscond from the tedium,
    proceed to Parliament Hill to watch them fly kites; trusting not to repose
    in a sniper's sights.

109

The Resurrection, Port Glasgow, of nineteen forty-five to forty-seven, is not the
    triumph that the late Referendum could have been.
Art can incorporate a summation of what we inherit to impart of national
    tradition. The tradition of the Clyde is now said to have died with Jimmy
    Reid.
A kind of colloquial good, 'Waking Up', 'Tidying', 'Reunion of Families'—
    nineteen forty-five–forty-seven bore an obligatory hope—can stitch
    together a public shroud from private kindness; so that political
    bloodymindedness must mourn its vital progeny born dead.
Scotland is not England, of course; and, of the two, the condition of England
    is worse. Spencer's was an English Muse, nonetheless; a power of sorts
    among her foreign peers; and with a very local sense of redress that,
    undeniably beautiful, pressed down on Clydesiders a sentimental appeal,
    like skeins of festal-coloured knitting wool, that they may well have
    wished not to possess.

110

Death, in Holbein, is an articulate quick skeleton, joined at times by its twin,
   skidding around and across the exemplary scene:

The Pope in his obligatory triple crown: Emperor Maximilian with righteous
   frown: the gourmand King of France in tastebud dalliance: the Empress
   caught procéssing: the Queen heard loudly protesting:

A Cardinal in state with his red wide-brimmed hat: a Bishop in a proper
   pastoral setting, about to resign both mitre and crozier; he seems unterri-
   fied by the meeting:

The Duke appears busier, but is haught and uncharitable; his councillors are
   feeble straw men. He is caught while turning in disdain from a poor
   woman distraught:

Death has seized the Abbot's robes in its clack-knuckled hand; they warp as if
   tugged by a gusting wind: the Abbess is a victim of violent crime:

The Nobleman, more violent than valiant, strives to resist with sword and fist
   his latticed assailant, but to no avail:

A Cathedral Canon, ambling to his stall, attended by his Fool, is intercepted at
   the door by a privy whisperer:

The unjust Judge will not be quit of Death's well-proven writ. He is struck to
   the ground, a last bribe in his hand, his wand of office broken. For him
   the hourglass has turned its final rote and justice has spoken: the
   Advocate is stopped in the street by someone importunate. A poor peti-
   tioner has been beaten to it. Death's coin mingles with that of the rich
   client. By nightfall, Advocate will supplicate but in vain:

The Senator looks to have trodden Death underfoot in his progress along the
   street. A poor man seeks a boon. Let him seek on. The Senator speaks
   only with his clients in power. A bat-winged imp with bellows squats at
   his ear. The prostrate cadaver is in good nick, shows us implements of its
   trade—hourglass and spade. I would describe the Senator's countenance
   as preoccupied rather than afraid:

The Preacher is an accomplished orator but Death is more eloquent still, with
   its terse Senecan style. In this scene Holbein has caught characteristic
   expressions particularly well: the Parish Priest, for all his many good
   works, is accosted as he walks. Nothing is so sacred that it must be
   spared. Even the very best are bonily scarecrowed:

The Skeletal Bloke restrains, by grasping cowl and cloak, the Monk who, mouth a round O, emits a silent howl of funk, endeavours cash-box in hand to do a bunk: the Nun, set among sin's clichés, eyes a trim young man in slashed doublet, fine hose, who returns her gaze. His lute is aslant on his lap in arty vaunt. Death is a gaunt maid pinching out their joint wick.

Commendably firm the Old Woman mocked in *dance macabre* by twin skeletons. One plays a type of xylophone, the other sports a floral crown. She stumps on. Though one grasps her arm she does not glance at them:

The Physician, who reads at his book, has to crick his neck as well-set Bones enters in the rôle of care-provider. He leads on a hobbling citizen, and has in charge a urine specimen, a vial as large as an ogre's bladder:

The Astrologer sits at his ornate desk in an ornate chair, wearing a rich robe; stares awkwardly at a pendant celestial globe. Bones, with twisty mock courtesy, proffers a skull, as if to a fellow professional in Faustian impudence:

The Rich Man's chamber is emphatically double barred, a cell. Death has possession of stool and pannier. He scoops up coins like roast chestnuts, and grins. The man, judged by headgear and feature, is a Jew. His arms make a farcical show of fear and outrage for all to enjoy:

The Merchant brings to display an everyday scene on a quay, its pattern-book items of ships' tackle crowding the sky. A prosperous churl, with root vegetable face, stoops to unlace a bale. Death takes him at once by the tail of his cloak and a haul of his hair. His fellow venturer scarpers in wailing, hands-flailing fear:

In *The Seaman* Death scrambles aboard, a sixteenth-century stuntman, or like a revenant, one of the undead. Holbein couldn't tell hawser from buntline; the ship is inaccurately drawn. It will soon go down and they will all drown, save one. They would have drowned anyway, even if Holbein had set a mastery of nautical engineering on display:

The Knight, in ceremonial armour, appears out of date. He is here, briefly, to whet Death's condign humour; he has been run through from small of back to groin, so that he seems to dance around the thick pizzle of his own lance:

The Count has been waylaid, or caught in a surprise raid, off guard and without armour. As with the death of the Knight, we catch the last breath of chivalry here. Does this refer to incidents in the Peasants' War? If that were Holbein's intent, surely he would have drawn a clearer allegorical moral from the event:

Though still obtruding a dulcimer—my 'xylophone'—on the scene, Death
deals gently enough with the Old Man. The grave is dug, even the lid is
prepared. Death steps around. With one more tread the old lad will be
dead in the ground. I am afraid; give me a hug:

The Countess tries on a new dress. Death is at her back, affixing a necklace of
malign luck to her throat: here see a fresh-wedded Lady walk with the
new bridegroom in sportful talk. Death gives its drum a festive whack:

The Duchess sits bolt upright in her bed, as though she has dreamed of dread.
Death wrests from her the large, thick coverlid. A second skeletal form
with rudimentary chin plays dire music on a violin. The quality of this
block is said to be especially fine:

Death pulls at the Pedlar's sleeve, as if haggling were not over with and he is
forbidden to leave. The man is desperate to be gone, angered by the
clutch of rude bone. A second Death's head provides absurd perch to a
tromba marina:

The Ploughman is as one blest; more fortunate even than the Parish Priest.
Death whips the old fellow's team towards a beautiful far-off gleam—at
once the setting sun, trust in redemption through Christ, and resurrec-
tion at the last:

The Child is spared nothing except—possibly—fear. It is a wretched hovel
and lacks a door. The mother cooks something on a small fire; the smoke
is peculiar, it appears a wraith. Death is brisk at the task. The Child
in its smock gives its mother a last look. These wretchedly poor folk
possess—most unlikely—an hourglass. This is Holbein, I would guess,
making his series click with a satisfying reprise:

His displays of poverty and of power abused are now, almost without excep-
tion, spectacularly well-housed. Intrinsic value is, as things now are, a
trade-off with valuation and milieu. *The Dance of Death* reserves a block
for the professional Fool, with a fool's bladder and all; though, in gaping
rags that expose a dangling tool, he resembles a 'natural' with leer and
drool. The Skeleton makes the pace at a run, its bagpipes scrawning
away with a lively tune. They are 'enjoying a joke', a yokel version of
folk in the *Tatler*, nothing subtler; and of course it's a ruse—the joke is
on the Fool and us; though that can't be the whole sum of Holbein's
theme or of Holbein's time.

III

Leicestershire parsons, rollypolled mired white wigs of wreathed winter kex
    blown over shorn fields in high winds that riotously mix, tumbling into
    fable like Reynard the Fox.

Good reason and no needed excuse in or out of season to squire or diocesan or
    yeoman or churl.

Grunty-headed pietas, gout's plenty, granted random port-quietus.

Just enough starchy orders to set off anarchy; notorious liaisons afforded
    monarchy by those who could afford little.

England belonged to itself in title merely, as kex stalks are brittle and rattle in
    thin throngs. And still but barely belongs.

Radicalism *passim*, as in *Rural Rides*.

The spirit never was a free thing; only the wind maybe at the autumn equinox
    or March Ides; and even then an illusion, self-persuasion in one of its
    several modes.

....

'Speechified at Wisbeach', that's Cobbett, least amiable great grandfather of
    the Hobbit; a vociferous anti-Semite of the same rut and truck as Pound,
    their hatred of Jews wrapped up with paper money, monopolies, stock-
    jobbing, fiddled revenues, expropriated land.

Slanders aside, I agree with much that they said.

Pound, at the end, admitted he had failed. And there was always, with Cobbett,
    a sense of having been jostled by the unruly, and ignobly foiled.

'To be victor is to have grasped and deployed a superior vector.'

Rhymes reduce the heterogeneous matter of the world to their own primes.

The poem is, in part, a diagram of the diaphragm not of my heart.

....

Paper money, though, was more Cobbett's fixation than it was Pound's caper.

When Ez said 'bureaucracy is destruction', he saw eighty years ahead, staked
    out poetry as finality's diction,

Jedermann's alienation from his own will becoming a ceremonial file of costly
    evidence.

Dichtung und Wahrheit is a matter of having to get bottom gear instinctively
    right from the start.

....

Instrumental, and yet as having a life to itself; and the matter not precisely
    divisible half and half, as in some cases it is easy enough to do. We are
    not here speaking of divorce, but of making a case for the separate exist-
    ence of a voice—'like to a tenement or pelting farm': words to which
    Cobbett might have been glad to set his name.
Do you have to be so aggressively recondite? I don't see why not.

112

As Holbein's *Dance of Death* may have appeared to Berne's religious connois-
    seurs and aesthetes of iconoclastic wars, so, in the Age of Aquarius,
    Rouault's *Miserere* exposes misery to occasion's profane sightseers.
For 'As' read 'Not as', and see *Note*.
Technic: in fact not Holbein's surrogate woodcut but copper plate. The effect
    of the squab lines is that of ink lavishly spilt with much care to obscure
    a repeated, never bettered, original fault; an acidic secret for the now
    impious secretariat to ferret out and to swank about as 'ascetic' art.
The impact overall is of trodden-in charcoal wet-scumbled on coarse
    wrapping-canvas. Sufferers resemble oil-coated convoy survivors, which
    is appropriate.
And tyranny is sealed into its dire ennui of self-parody, each held-unhealed
    betrayal formal as an ode.
Four plates imitate Holbeinian skeletal horridry as a type of emotive lever
    commanding the dry eye. All four are in the section 'War' which, for me,
    too straitly narrows the score.
Rouault has more compassion than had Holbein for his dead men up and down
    the line; friend and foe, lumpen as they come from the Somme-Flanders
    grimpen where common duty flounders forward to fatal blunders and
    belated pity.
Carnality is spectral; the redemptive divinity of Christ conjectural; though not
    to Rouault.

113

When I dwelt in Massachusetts for my sins, skunk-musk I found a not-unpleasant scent, wafting in around dusk from distant areas of bins. Raccoons, who appear to wash their paws when they dip for trash but who stand their ground and look you in the eye, I did not care for in their domestic proximity.

After a final sleepover in McLean, I am barely competent to judge things American: as emblem of comity the malign comet-eye of Salem my sign.

Alienation, alienhood: nothing that I can write here is datum. That is understood. Each late hymn a form of votive offering to establish an uncertain claim.

But I am glad, now, taking to this strange English fen country that grants me slow entry and its bleak decorum.

114

Happy the tears that are not camera-shy and haemorrhage to cheers.

Bomberg did portraits rarely, self-portraits queerly. He could have produced them in-style and lived well.

To the realm of ideas a spendthrift thriftiness: a verb or Berkeleyan particle— Berkeley on optics being Bomberg's oracle.

Approve him according to the likes of Blake's *Jerusalem*. Why? People self-maim, irrespective of injury. The cry you have just uttered has not heard of you, trust me.

Adjuncts of weight and mass rebuilding the dead face without cause.

I have known a gifted, gracious man so saturate in sweet white wine that his skin stank like a sodden nappy as he sank slowly to type. His slurred tongue needed to be frequently wrung. A man of the word, utterly without spite, dissolving into his own detritus, hapless poetry slithering off his lap and through a fatal pedestrian gap, as in Gin Lane, that exemplary scene.

The dirty matter of moral freedom needs to be visited again; when what we have is the polity of Sodom and that other city of the plain.

115

The Chinese written character for *pivot*, with its High Modernist clout, has at its heart a style of handmade nail struck by my long-stranded plebeian kin of whom, courtesy Ruskin, I am inordinately proud.

On Romanesque tympanum Samson, sinew-strapping youth, durst wrench the lion's mouth to gape-a-grin mask, ready for Tate and Lyle whose traditional green and gold tins have style, though nothing to equal the 'beehive' of a nice naive girl or 'I'm backing Britain' on a Union Jack milk carton gone in a seasonal flurry of bank-skirl.

116

At Nash, by Knill, tucked into its English pocket under the half-Welsh hill:

The night wind bearing a heavy louche load of terrene sound, an intermittent slosh and rattle of rain that sheers off again, to isolation, it seems, but in grand fettle.

I said once of her no-nonsense mind: it can command presence even as I cast to apprehend its tense gist.

So too with these cross-directional forces: there is something beyond the mêlée that one foresees; distress being an ancient right of way through the ruined parkland of original joy.

117

In general it is the umbelliferae to which we affix the term kex, that is to say, dead wintry stalks of the same. In common lore, hemlock and cow-parsley share the common grame. See Amphlett and Rea, *The Botany of Worcestershire* (Birmingham, nineteen-o-nine) secure in repute if not fame.

I looked to inure us against attack; had recruited that wayfaring fighting cock, as much a bigot as any squire or clerk in a wig yet stout champion of the poor man and his pig. Minutely observant, he, of broadly changing 'nature' and all things untowardly.

Fatalities—you will have heard—lately incurred from the poisonous root of a poem miseaten as horseradish or with rabbit in a pie-dish. Absurd way to die (my word!), nastily, unreadied, disbelieving.

Clare in his time took many another name, and a dream-wife, from grief and obscure shame.

Hemlock in particular will allure us to its black, indurated stare. This does not mean we should condone postures of abject craving, or project reinforced self-believing prayer.

The rare best were ever fated; the worst fêted; the rest scare-baited; berated by full malinquiry held under some bald acronym of our time.

Therefore repeal self-blame as Cobbett did, riding well the swell of ill-fame; and as Clare did not, grown a stout simpleton in the Northampton portrait. Pre-frontal lobotomy fashionable much later. Clare's countenance appears to anticipate it, albeit caught by an amateur.

118

Straight narrative may be possible if obliquely applied. Plot not the forte.
  Begriff has import; the laugh is on risible grief.
She snapped her fingers; the candles at once became flame-capped, steadied
  their dance. They will see out Advent if not the ever-impending worship
  of ignorance and dark matter.

....

'It comes at you from all angles and with the false tongues of angels.'
Who was it said, 'Thee gives me a pain'? And in which scene? And in what
  cinema did your waters break and your womb bleed?
It is a bare five days to the Feast of the Nativity—as we reckon—and every
  known national cavity is stuck with cloves for fear it may sicken earlier
  than the New Year.
Nor can you now have access to Weeping Cross with what you know, despite
  the absence of widely promised, heavily threatened, snow.

119

Ante- and post-partum 'combination of powers in an unknown substratum'.
  What a theme! Or this, 'a man may die twice, thrice, a day; be in a state
  of annihilation, that is to say'.
Bravo, Berkeley! 'Reality of bodies' spoken about in such a way!
Circa nineteen sixty-three the British Council, to its credit without fee, taught
  me to tape-edit: razor blade—you sliced diagonally—chinagraph pencil;
  slow coûture with spool and reel.
From then on, at once magician and dupe, I could set up single-track solipsism
  by forward-backward spasm and endless loop.
It has been a fair while; finds me on the right side of senile and a mean recorder
  of the *funkblätter* scene:
Even now can recall where I last saw Berkeley's spare keys to the code.
Still, some may need to read the above as a parody ode; a mode to restyle and
  redeliver public order.

120

If Gogol had contrived 'Peer Gynt' as a Mussorgsky libretto, might that work's
    stature now be greater than the Commendatore's statue or *Sprachgitter*?

What a question when, sometime soon, the assembled dead daybooks will have
    come to resemble the detritus of Camp Bastion rather than Anselm
    Kiefer's various deconstructions of Celan.

Who is that jealous god of whom you swore we were well rid? Is he the one who
    did those clever leaden books you can stand for ever to read?

At the vertiginous epicentre of high verse, I could concede, I am especially
    conscienceless; but also driven perforce by the dense noise in my ampli-
    fier which she said must be similar to the 'roaring on the floor of the
    Bourse' that some understand as the fulcrum of the unprofound cul-
    tural anarchy of this latter time, the *funksturm of réclame*, all the better
    to perform its exclusively celibate (does he mean sterile?) game.

121

Demonstrable progress towards my diploma requires the poem to be worked
    up from its ground bass with a convincing power of climb. Otherwise art
    is a misnomer.

Milton was an able musician and understood that; and that vowels and
    consonants and stress blend in a tendresse weighed with 'order service-
    able' well-becoming the power to summon.

'The valley of the Teme re-endowed each spring with comfortable trim wildness
    and ready fable confirms my belief in the credibility of eternal life.'

More than one lone rich man has drowned in his own pond watched over by
    a swan.

Milton and the Italian Cities was meant to be more than a gazetteer-treatise.
    Alternative polities are ponderable issues before they become landfill
    and vernacular-style executive houses.

122

The winter sky at noon, grey-fawn; the mistletoe brimming to be smitten down.

They say that I make too much of mistletoe. True; though I'm not now, nor ever was, an adherent of the Golden Bough; even as I see the Thuringian forest, never tamed, merely temporarily becalmed, gently pass by:

Small onion-domed church on a hill, an incense and praise receptacle that is memorable, that I would do well to recall.

Those taught to tell it how it is will have a surprise when at last they must meet their electronic mimesis pitting cross against nought, checking the kama sutra positions of thought-genesis; inspiration's nemesis.

If dialectic had not, before you were born, made its qualitative leap from pedagogical tactic to political structure, you might now enjoy a simple return upon nature, be at ease with the paratactic subordinate disarray.

123

Brecht wrote the poem which people now acclaim—'Of poor B.B.'—on the night train back to Augsburg from Berlin.

I have ridden that route while a winter evening shut down the farms in Thuringia; and an occasional shrine topped with a small spiked onion; and a nameless town.

Time kept quietly to itself; I adapted to its whim; read some *Peer Gynt* followed by a half-attentive stint on the judicial murders in Plötzensee where I had set my wreath to die the death together with bits of official new myth rotted by weather; and votive messages left for some obscured motive almost certainly decent; and wanky candles that looked recent.

At this distance I say: why is epic remembrance still a half-furtive remnancy; and why are we who mourn *de iure* such con men?

I stayed on past Augsburg, got out at München.

'I, B.B., was displaced from the forest, the *ur-Wald*, together with the mother who bore me; but remain its child.' Something like that. He became a brat and a poet; and a survivor of the cold, although he was not old when he died.

I admire what he wrote more than I respect his laureate career which, in that familiar DDR-way, was reprehensible, though no more criminal than the activity of a goat.

In a minor-major rôle he reminds me of Thomas Cromwell—duplicitous to work good, and whatever it may mean to serve one's time well in the glare and shadow of a degenerate public mode, heretics as friends, the Stasi at the stage-door.

....

'Vom Tod im Wald'; among the early best, 'Death in the Forest' is prime—that being also an alchemical term. And poetry is alchemy, did I say?

See this poem perform a kind of Brueghelish *ritterkind* routine: 'Then they rode swiftly away across the plain', having brusquely buried one of their own.

That it is set in a non-existent pioneer bit of the Mississippi Valley is neither here nor there, except to the pedant's denigratory sextant.

The original version stood in his first play, the minatory *Baal*. It was set by Kurt Weill.

Form *in tempore destruendi* and *in ano mundi* casts itself upon its own quandary: either do things blindly, scrabbling for the late norm, or sustain the intractable, as indeed Brecht can, by maintaining—merely, so it will seem—the popular fable even in the face of populist alarm.

....

Naive opportunist Galileo baldly declares that the spheres twist and run while the sun steers.

'Can you confirm?' wires Vatican. Galileo (silly man!) says yes and does himself long-lasting harm.

House arrest with intellectual fasting and scrutiny of any future mss. is a generous compromise for someone so unwise.

He is looked after, in the tedium of his leper's squint-on-the-cosmos room, by a lucked-out daughter.

Creation speaks its second language in arrears; it is responded to with relieved laughter and renewed fears.

If original genius is to be graded, then I suppose that Kopernik can squat slightly higher in the chronological stack; but both were needed, and, some aver, each was divinely guided by his personal star.

....

Die stumme Katrin; die Dulle Griet; for these, but not for these alone, Brecht gave his words campaign feet.

And, no doubt, in *The Meeting at Telgte*, it is for them that Grass plies his commissary wit.

Each is indebted to the mute and the mad for the roof over his worldly head. Pity is a formality.

I do not so state facts to condemn them 'unter den namen' but merely to condense, if that makes sense.

That we are such gainers from the lottery losers, the loners, the self-soiled solitary dossers, the victims of military crimes, must give us pause even as new theatres open their wombs.

This is of course the *ad infinitum* game in which blame finally vanishes up the arse of the Muse.

. . . .

Why should the Union of Italian Railwaymen put on *The Trial of Lucullus*?

Dali's anagrammatic name, Avida Dollars, consummates our time. *Brecht ist nicht gerechtfertigt*. Shakespeare was a bad landlord. I cannot read or write German. Where is the harm? Nominate truth by youth plebiscite.

The harm is not yet any place where I might step aside to dice, though by now an item in the parallel cosmos where Lucullus, a triumphal general, is held suspended between passive Shadowland and active hell by a juror's appeal to the cherry tree brought back one year to Italy and planted there.

. . . .

Brecht names Brueghel's *Dulle Griet* a 'great war painting'; sees the woman herself as a domestic fury with 'the features of a servant' managing to save her few items of kitchenware and household property; but, like a landsknecht, with an eye to more. She has been called by someone a 'looter' which would suit her well enough. Indeed, she looks wall-eyed with fear or greed, a kind of insane rage her goad.

Brecht is thinking in terms of *Mother Courage*; but that prescriptive norm of description scarcely suits the disruption of natural order in Griet's world. Such is an insurrection of demons that prey on demons: the language of the learned Civilians, or even of the friars' sermons on the Fall, does not accommodate it at all.

The Thirty Years' War must have come near to what we are forced to see here. The monstrousness of the slaughter would fall within the parameter of peasant dancing and laughter and skating on animal bones, and mating behind barns, and be all the more terrible for that; but some would survive and keep sane. In *Griet*, God himself is mad or, worse, smilingly inane; or else he mutates and his present whereabouts are as yet unknown.

He could, I imagine, be that unrecognizable man under the blazing wall in Shoe Lane; but I would be too slow to explain and he'd be gone again before you know. Len Rosoman knew, though.

I don't engage well with language. It takes me over—no, not 'as a lover'. As a cuckoo plants its progeny on some feathered sucker. I hatch its meanings and naively imagine them mine.

That is why I react so extravagantly to Brecht; he too is like a landsknecht; like the Feldprediger in *Mother Courage*; like any millionaire arch-beggar; some such *sammelsurium* of amoral forage, a farrago.

Let me rephrase: less cuckoo; more toucan, macaw, cockatoo, birds of dire wisdom in a disguise of ventriloquism, raucous patter, cosseted spatterers of the West-Ost Diwan.

124

You may not expect me to say this after such a recital, but it is vital that we
 resurrect Brecht.

It is either him or politic Classic FM 'immortalizing' ephemera. Things have
 become that extreme and that reductive.

The turnip and bloater paste features exposed on programmes about benefits
 'shames', though they are indeed charmless, set off the wrong alarms
 and attract misdirected invective from our lobbies of phobias.

And that Brecht in some degree sold out his intellectual and moral pedigree
 for what he could get makes him all the more a fit object of study, with
 Nobodaddy and Noddy and just about everybody.

It is too late for us to desire virtue. We must make do with *Trauerspiel* and
 Brecht and *Baal* and Hollywood and piecemeal self-betrayal like snot on
 a fingernail.

125

That there is complex perjury in simple disavowal, from the first to the fourth
 estate, we take to in the *Histories* and the morality of surprise which
 Brecht calls alienation:

The syntax of justice—I don't care how you read me on this—and then
 the Gaultree betrayal—in the guise of Christian enterprise as per the
 homilies, internal assonance a skeletal upstarting adverse prance.
 Apocalyptic Dürer I advance.

Equivocation yet in season and not all disreputable since faith is treason.
 Brecht did not have that recourse, being on somewhat vulgar terms with
 his Muse though without that salutary distrust which is more rare, as in
 the best sonnets of Shakespeare or some end-of-tether Cavalier; or, of
 course, Father Southwell, that saint of courteous but steely dissent,
 whose soul was ever at the knife's point of self-attaint, though in truth
 he had no cause to fear God's Wrath.

Unequal equities, these, about which it is best not to sentimentalize.

126

Poem as Samson dozing post coitus with coiffure of unshorn hair.

Poem as Samson with shaved head, enslaved, blindly led, belatedly back on form.

Poem as classified information regarding élite of nation swimming with pigs in the Bahamas: a wealth of *Stimmung*, 'to which only the truly great belong'.

Poem as 'mutual comfort, the one to the other', barely attainable even with dual purpose spanner found in every well-managed home.

Poem as calorific oven; the moon as manipulator of the nervous system.

Poets with old-fashioned encyclopedic knowledge bring good seed to tillage.

I doubt that many since Rimbaud would so demand; though MacDiarmid and Pound could each make out a case in face of abuse by those with and without political bias, many of whom are of sound mind.

That there is a gnostic element in the firmament I am broadly persuaded though I do not push it to the extent that they did.

Poem as cradle of the unbiddable name.

A novice poet will tend to over-exploit the clarinet.

Poem as sitcom. Poem as labour at a seam.

These arpeggios are run off before the passacaglia's bass emerges, if it ever does.

127

No further to claim a gesture, the posture of an imposture, where I long pleaded my brief in conduct of our brief claim—thát being the poem as pure *geste* and ethical compass and my own double: I would not wish upon you the same degrees of trouble.

Gnosis of enterprise more and more treated as serious discourse. Flâneurship of entrepreneurship mysterious even to the wise.

Go into the street, hire the first few dozen you chance to meet; matters would be no worse. Business is cozen, so Wat the Tiler says—meaning various treasures of the common realm transmogrifying under the nation's eyes into a strange guise of fertile exilic calm.

128

Poem as gathered samphire, source of that 'dreadful trade' in Edgar's tirade
with regard to the void.

Poem as neuro-linguistic programme with close attachments to the absurd.

Poem in memoriam the Scipionic Circle or perhaps some other phantom
cénacle.

Goebbels, and a few einsatzgruppen chiefs, were run-of-the-mill intellectuals
with DSc's and DPhil's.

Some fiends indisputably have trained minds; are capable of domestic
kindness.

Who says now that divine philology enables the soul to judge well? I once
thought you could move so at will and with a good style.

The imposition of ashes not one of the spurious fetishes, or so I inform the
curious before curiosity wearies.

I am still a coherent fool with a cool idyll: the nitrate grove that excites and
fixates love.

Poem produces and delivers its changeable pantomime; pisses this time
serenely front stage into the orchestrage; delivers well a Handel aria,
with tact re-adjusts drunken tiara to good effect.

129

Poem as prime enforcer of the realm. Poem as hostage to straws that overwhelm.

Give me back the stocky *tu quoque* of the baroque.

Poem as slow burning arquebus fuse in a re-enactment universe.

Poem as nightmare stepmother in the Brothers Grimm. Poem as loquacious
sightseer at an unspeakable crime.

Poem reluctant to give its true name even though lately granted immunity
from recrimination.

Poem at home under its figtree and with a thriving pigsty.

Poem as hapless amateur in competition with 'Summertime'.

130

Slaughter of Innocents to accompaniments of laughter as at social events.

The barn owl, registered inaudible over a measured mile, performed in style. More than one small creature harmed. The whole exquisitely filmed. Equity is unstable. *Je est un autre* applies only to us; a writ of weight.

Claus von Stauffenberg, late acolyte of Stefan George, gave credibility to the old rogue by dying on the 'right' side for 'sacred' Germany. *Das Neue Reich* had meant to him both hierarchy and hegemony, as it so easily could for you and me, spiritualizing our self-esteem.

Harold Alexander, top-notch step dancer and Great War troop commander, one day did a solo turn to cheer his remnanted men after yet another clueless and rotten affray of wire and crater. His gift had not been forgotten even a century later.

. . . .

Britten composed *A Ceremony of Carols* in the bowels of a refrigerator ship. The *Axel Johnson* is not on anyone's honour-roll, so far as I can tell, but it ought to be. Retroactively entertain the captain to a one-and-three? The convoys were hard fought, often with understrength escort; and the U-boats methodically clocked up their kills for Goebbels' propaganda newsreels.

131

Prelude and first vocal ensemble of *Macbeth*, voices and instruments working to resemble imprisoned dogs barking at some premonition of death— this my own aural distortion merely—they intone so direly, the weird sisters: bad words in their pale bladders of death, Verdi.

Genius is not so unlike being dense.

Is this the ridiculous price I have been eager to pay for your praise?

'It is chance if it includes life', said puckish Allison. And again I am in debt to a book by a dead young man which I shall be charged for by those who have behaved well under fire.

Obsession is repetitious when it is not mute.

132

Of course Desnos is one of my heroes; and Celan another: who was a hand-
some man; who seriously hit on bereft Ingeborg, her well-heft complici-
tous moan.

In the domain of popular fable *Dracula* is more enjoyable and more spectacular.

One rescues Desnos again from his sacrificial carelessness towards all orders
befehlshaberisch, and occupational sordors.

And I still tremble for them, those SOE women. Give me something atrocious
to be repaired over time, smilingly, entirely without shame; to which
I may shamelessly attach my theme.

Do not forget to submit my overtime claim.

133

'Mystery', back there, as in Abhorson the executioner, 'fie upon him, he will
discredit our—— '.

A head falls, to steam in the icy straw: there is no significant rise in oligarchical
acclaim for some gut-smeared lout of the law.

The swordsman from France who detached Anne's head was a delicate trick-
ster, it quickly appeared. He stood her the short measure of a dance, well
meriting the purse he received for his pains.

English poetry, put to the test, acknowledges that things are so—such bloody
elegance in sight of, in spite of, raven and crow; 'save' for some churl's
get, wits thrawn, rootling in the raw straw-paste, hoping—fat chance!—
for a headsman's dropped coin, to let him grin and begin snortling,
as for a bit of blessèd martyr's bone.

134

Genius is inimical to the *grex* but not to the *gens*. I say this as *senex*, not even to tax poets barely out of their teens, or tease those loves to whom I am now ex-.

Rooks and jackdaws roost together in weighty flocks; telepathic each neighbourly twitch and scritch; then the barbarous massed cry intensifying the bereft night sky: a strange omission until now from my gnostic theodicy.

If dark nature were simply a spread feature, a cover for the eery silences of wartime Worcestershire and other hinterlands of that legendary nation, mere meditation would be done by now. But, into the finalities of my eighties, I cannot let ill alone.

It is, in Guderian's good phrase, 'the revenge of reality' upon mere politic mysticality that may require my metre to engage with and cry pause.

I know very well the spectacle I need to be seen to perform: like riding a one-wheel bicycle while standing on the shoulders of a more stable man.

Those who urge this charge have a strong case, despite all that it denies and overlooks. One cannot have read—I imagine—so many great books with 'how true' pencilled neatly in the margin and still be considered a wise virgin.

It is as if I had said, at one time or another, 'I expose my dead on a platform for the elements and hordes of the air to consume'.

So much for a belief system in which words have become demi-gods.

135

Poem as scimitar-curve, shear along sheer, a 'Tribal' class destroyer, veteran of the North Cape run, bearing down on a submarine that has struck and already gone from the scene, leaving sea-rubble wretchedly a-swim, thickslicked in oil.

Rapid hapless signal flags, the merchantmen's red rags, warp and snatch on the Arctic wind. Frantic asdic, its wiped mind becoming, with old memory and new writing, something forlornly grand.

Poem as wall map or table chart of a desperate, remote, protracted bid to escape. Poem in due time a diminished aide-mémoire to vanished strategic priorities of fire.

Poem as equity release—whatever that is.

Poem as no less an authority on history than whom?

136

Poem plies admittance to gnosis as to an exclusive dance among species.

I am not, meanwhile, proposing to run this thing with the thermometer scale
at twenty, thirty, degrees below freezing in hostile seas:

But to be kingmaker; genius-backer, taker-up of the dude, the crude no-hoper.
To be mediocrity's factor:

To enjoy much loved celebrity in the soap opera of contemporary poetry.

Your *echt heldenherr*: for all I know this could be the attitude of Brecht, to
whom also I am beholden, here and elsewhere, for my (not all that secret)
bit on the side.

We avoided—evaded—the army. I was my own enemy.

We acquired pelf, making the poor our metaphor. But he made vastly more
than I grubbed for myself.

Poem as posthumous running sore.

137

Plush, that others appeared to find pleasant even if old-fashioned, set my skin
to frissonate with its dense poisonous moss of purple-red stings. So did
a three-piece suite of bristly moquette in the best room at the back of
the house, for which we had little use, where the wind-up gramophone
held state.

I was a haptic, not a happy, boy.

Some kids had irons on their legs like *drogues*, whereas I could leap seven
leagues without impediment.

The faint transparent scent of snow in its descent, shriving that small child,
returns to him now if it return at all.

Not even the thirty-seven species of the bird of paradise are admitted to
heaven.

138

'How our torpedo boats would clear an enemy boom in time of war': a quaint picture-postcard I would otherwise have to invent depicts that sublime action like something from Mr Wells's fiction.

But by that date—around nineteen eight—the torpedo boat was becoming obsolete; the 'torpedo boat destroyer' its ruthless, well-graced heir.

There cannot have been even a rogue rumour of Darwin in our naval design between nineteen ten and nineteen sixteen, what with those misbegotten battlecruisers fatally in vogue.

Idiot data, clung-to as to an explosion-flung spar, is saecular folly.

Jackie Fisher, ideologue, could not abide delay. Jellicoe, smitten with tactical melancholy, was ever too slow in manoeuvre.

Decorum is required of a forum even though it predict doom. Talk of the jury 'still being out' is the euphemism for that, and does not disturb any tectonic plate grinding towards a great schism. Contain your fury.

'Take me to Addenbrooke's; I have a subscription there.'

139

Music of Hungary, even when angry and mourning, retains what is incorrigibly sturdy in the churning hurdy-gurdy: that is a good augury, provided what I say about it is true; it may not be. I am like a man with one shoe; don't ask me why: I would still lay claim to your critical esteem.

In poetry, ignorance can sometimes work things to the good, as a form of muse-induced narcolepsy in which, entranced, you retain evidence of the tombs among which you have danced: *mots, êtes-vous des mythes et pareils aux myrtes des morts?*

I would (yet again) cite Desnos as witness; but, then, creatively he was both profound and shrewd; his word of mouth was neither tipsy nor the slurry of a grand mood; far and away the best of those Surreal men sunbathing in the shadow of the Sorbonne.

Poem as questionable item in a cultural film of established acclaim.

In so acquiring themes I am the Jackdaw of Rheims (when in France pronounce [ʁɛ̃s]).

140

'L'hymne de l'Union Européenne', an elevation of hereditary Enlightenment
platitude made to perform as would a grand convoy filmed in broad
oceanic imperturbable ride, oil tankers at its heart, destroyers and
corvettes on either side.

Voice-over by Barrault, Cocteau; Fischer-Dieskau; or by Olivier who recited
history liked a baffled lover with a crib, though its well-formed cliché
could have been performed, without too much redaction, by—let us
say—Pétain in launching Vichy as his supreme parable.

When you need to rake out the caked shit with your fingers it soon gets rid of
any reticence that lingers; and you decide to swagger a bit like the old
gunslingers.

Pétain and Péguy: both of peasant stock. In nineteen forty a malign minority
took the one for the other, an error inherent in the cult of duty, though
this does not excuse the fault.

Poetics itself a utile caucus, once, of wooden cities, akin to the Hanseatic ports.

We brought Lübeck to ruin with a mischievous spark, a flick to its old stack of
beauties, as if so doing were topmost of civilization's sporting duties;
whereas it was a prime experiment in branding a fire-storm with its
newly perfected name, as inspiration consummated by the perfect poem.

The imagination suffers annulment; neo-liberal satiety becomes its imaginary
coffers.

Chorus of drones and special forces, and special offers, and scorched bones.

141

That Fairfield decoy site on the flight path to Birmingham was never set
adequately alight.

During those epic times a few bombs were hastily decanted by some unheroic
crew onto precious cucumber frames and the like.

The immense black holly trees between us and Wildmoor were a cavernous
preserve of bones from a primal war; some even from the Mercian Ark.

To compose an obsolescent metaphysical poem is a bit like fusing or defusing
a small museum-proud bomb; but more resembles drifting backwards
among spheres, bearing an indeterminate claim, undocumented, none-
theless indelibly in your name.

142

Ordered re-appearance of ideas from chaos: motto-phrase for poiesis of my
    declared period but not since.

Poem as 'dome of many-coloured glass' caught in mid-explosion on slow-
    motion film.

Barely in memory a ceremonial and normal life that can contain grief for a
    dead wife.

Imagination, at such and such a putsch, a form of conservative agitation. In an
    unjust nation. *Freitod* its safest ambition.

This is not a creed. Nor is it quite yet an autopsy on public need.

When ingenuity is suppressed let it not be disordinately released, or we shall
    all be gassed by a watercolourist of scant ability and poor taste.

Delete and substitute:

'For the first time in our history, love for the Führer has become a legal term'.

And not even this will discredit our mystery before the highest democratic
    posthumous consistory, our wounds shallow, our tears glistery.

Poem as compact design, supreme nadir in the trap of a drain. Poem as dwarfed
    and distorted mimeo, disseminating in rhyme the murderous bibles as if
    they were Berlin or Warsaw or Moscow bus timetables.

Had Britain 'gone under' in that dire frame I would, a decade later, have
    become a Home Fires collaborator, I shouldn't wonder; but through fear
    rather than greed.

143

As we were sitting near the Landwehrkanal, weaving a morose ballad around
Rosa and Karl, for no good lexical reason I interrupted mysel'.

Cynical Gottfried Benn, that exemplary poet, could dissect his own mortglut
as if it were the sex of a prostitute, then tamper with the clinical report.

Bertolt Brecht had as much tact as any other brutalist architect, O my brother.

'Lightning Inside the Ash Cloud: an Ode.'

Discharge of afflatus embitters the waters in a revival of the Star Wormwood.

Property is propriety—vide OED—and is so appropriated by the various theo-
dicies of greed.

Most poets are less capable than those who at airports x-ray our tits and our
boots and happily leave us to scrabble.

Whether I maintain anything the Augsburger would wish to corroborate I am
content that you table as a matter debatable. He did once state that
Brueghel deals in contradiction; with the suggestion that it is this which
renders him great.

Some of his own actions seem a bit less than straight: the Augsburger's,
I mean. But was he not plagued by demokratisches rat tushes? He must
have been. What was it he reneged upon?

144

British coastal waters—north Cornwall, Ulster—are reefed and neckleted
with wrecked U-boats, their hulls by now merely rust-bolls and similar
sprouts of metallic canker; each one a depth-diver's fetish, whose
activities further scruff the greenish-reddish sea-bottom scurf.

On camera no filleted bones appear; in some ways a relief though 'closure' may
be denied grief. Maybe there truly are none—bones—to be shown; but
check lens then screen.

Ancient accusations of inhumanity seem, in the interim, to have been infor-
mally reconciled between the nations. Tenderly treated, the near-senile
survivors, and why not? All who appear are welcome to cast a wreath at
some otherwise indistinguishable spot, see it totter on the water, a for-
lorn jot: even disbelievers in life after death—there will be those among
such out-of-breath reivers as we have got here.

I admit to wearing the rote sorrow like a dark suit.

Further, my Muse of national demise—by now a self-perpetuating sacred
unholy farce like Burton's *Melancholy*—is a sow in farrow.

145

Locus of focus in the re-orientation of poor jokes.

Stet an abiding regret: not having invited the late Michael Bentine to dine tête-à-tête. We would have made weird noises while we ate.

But—oy veh!—the miserdom of the world's wisdom; the dreary faubourg of Malfoy, as timebound as in Rouault's *Miserere*.

Affording the proletariat opportunity and power to govern the state, no matter that they may not know or care what they are at: this, I imagine, is what Brecht was about. Otherwise—I believe he said or implied—freedom is an affront, a libertine-reactionary vaunt.

I would of course hold the over-bold to account.

That line of Melville—'The hemlock shakes in the rafter, the oak in the driving keel'—you can feel the impartial wilfulness of language engage with its nature to be both active and still, and thereby at one with the Divine Will...

Up and down like a porpoise and with as mysterious a purpose.

146

Commemorating the young Auden who all too early became old, I angrily mourn that vain slippered pantaloon with the awesome name.

The Orators oversteps the years, our frustrate rage foretold.

'Banks make payments in fairy gold.' I was a babe but not, I imagine, immune to bribe, when the great poet wrote that.

Poesis is chaos theory for the unmathematical, one may suppose.

'Twigs as varied bent' came this way in my angry anglo-immured twenties as prologue to an American advent of versing rogues, the vague and improvident. I did not know then what the words meant and still don't.

147

Of Hemingway's short stories taught to sophomore nurses in Ann Arbor, after fifty-six years I retain only this: *Otro loco más*. How ridiculous the serious labour of virtuous series without right aim towards end and free witness!

So much for 'esemplastic power' with now a skim of plastic dross from shore to ocean rim: yet where, some sudden time, the storm petrels make their swift low pass, revert to climb, as shadows briefly magnified by sun through spindrift-rime.

148

Genius has the ease to wear contradictory faces; is not shamed by public
   display of its crises. The Muse it almost invariably makes of things
   obtuse, gross—does it matter terribly?

Intense concentration and utter indifference lie on each side of a psychic
   equation undemonstrable as equivocation, a ruse.

Je est un autre: the little rotter was quite right, of course.

The refracted covenant, arc-spray, observed moment by moment against the
   Atlantic's deep-cloven slant; the twin Oerlikon on its mount, depth
   charges beerbarrelling in cloned count:

The obduracy to reject knowledge, resist wisdom and other such obligations of
   political freedom; the manifold implications.

The morality of radical surprise that Brecht terms alienation, exploding in the
   convoy's wake with or without contact, as if for commotion's sake.

149

Ruck in shock release, shot gross down iron and brick chute—

As a kenning this has some meaning—it is a beginning—

Paid for with money out of a teapot on the mantelpiece if there was any.

I greet what is serflike in me without enmity. *Geffe iuvat* adequately suggests
   both stake and state. With it I make my bequests.

Publica vox dicit, leges quod mammona vicit.

Propriety of owning property. Chartism the great schism. Nicely, thank you.
   Age of the Banker. But yet elect Abdiel; let him outrank you and be wise.
   Such is free will.

Wat the Tiler, John the Red Nose, Francis Feeble the woman's tailor: irregular,
   out of a hat heroes in parlous times. Not that anything here cries *Dismas*;
   but we are not your rabble and never were.

The Gospel of Mark unreasonably stark. A dumb to-do of women fearful
of omen.

That unnamed witness clad only in a linen cloth who ran away naked: is it his
word we take for it? Even that | teeters on the revoked; attracts editors.
Brevity is not neatness. Scared could be sacred.

A priest I know well | asperges her Easter flock with a wristy flick from a bowl.
She too invokes Mark, the stone tipped aside like a sacrilegious joke; the
midmost vacuity of things impenetrably dark...

Condoms and needles littered among the tombs.

We speak with difficulty. Grammar coarse even if not faulty (that double nega-
tive in the Greek).

....

The denial of landed property to the gross of the people sets the constitution
in jeopardy, urged Edmund Burke, from whom Chartism could be said
to have descended.

O Tory-grandee-right-to-buy oligarchy, plutocratic malarkey, Uncle Toby and
Tristram Shandy real ale, in which and wherefrom we are all grounded
awash, thriftlessly and for sale.

In childhood I knew Dodford: the planned idyll, four acres and a cow, a small
plum harvest, some of which you would be able to sell, perhaps from a
roadside stall.

Was there not, in the instance of O'Connor, a degree of managerial naivety
tantamount to misdemeanour?

Need we choose between the Gospel of Mark, Edmund Burke, or even Ross
Poldark when we do homage to the great who cogitate the human condi-
tion of aggro and inanition? Or should the palms, the alms, be bestowed
on Coram's Hospital, as old Handel did in his best Handelian style,
thanks be to God?

....

No upright poem in its uptight English can seem to me quite free from
limescale under the rim.

150

'Balsam', in India, is the name given to *Impatiens*, of which there are numerous
variants in all their glory among the Nilgiri Hills, where Alun's spirit
haunts, one complicitously feels.

Read this not quite as you would a short story.

To conclude 'time heals' may be because there is need of a rhyme; something
trite comes along and you lack the nous to refuse it. We are wounded
souls and overesteem verse.

A man with such heed to demonstrate tactical worth does not commit suicide
an hour before combat in which he would usefully acquit himself to death.

I concede his melancholy and his guilt. The Welsh nation; the ruin, five years
in, of that first Labour administration, could have done for him eventu-
ally with minimal sin. But that he engineered a slovenly demise on the
sly, that I will deny.

The letters from India are as intelligent as Keats about politics and the poet;
and not one whit randier. But everything sinks into the sand here and
I must admit to blinking back unpoetical tears, particularly for Gweno
who outlasted him by more than seventy years that compounded every
species of Welsh arrears.

....

Suppose him a survivor of torture, tripwire or Burma fever. Eventually, though
accident-prone, he would, I believe, have made more money than James
Hanley ever did with *Grey Children* or *The Welsh Sonata*.

Seren—my Welsh is poor—has to mean star. It could just as well have been
swan; anything I would prefer it to mean.

Poem as mongoose and snake wallah. Fine out there. Not wanted in the same
bedroom with us at home, I can tell.

In Cwmaman no forty-part *Amen*; nor at Mountain Ash; nor up in Aberdare.

I cannot cut a dash anymore with music's ideal choir on the hill of heavenly
spoil, in the screenstruck vale of dole.

Nor could Alun finally out-talk sleek half-alien Rilke; not with a wired-on grin,
an inaudible black Bible-joke.

....

Whatever turns on demonstrable probables must revert to origins of tort.

Time will disclose, eventually, the purpose of dark matter in the universe, but not to us nor to our personalized Creator devoid of spark:

Though time itself is a creature of the primal blackstuff and is here called into being by the mechanical nature of theme and other ephemera:

The aspen's full shivery delight, small aerial pool to the sight; hawthorn quick again, luminous chalk-white; once-rare red kite a now familiar livery, a hawk's veer, its flair in flight.

Poem to restart pumping-system for self-esteem sewage and rage of heart.

'The restlessness and the scattered gift'; a vowing of unity. We live through inanity and craft.

Buried in Burma the serried long bones miscarried.

Poem as honeycomb, as hidden cleft in the *cwm*; as claim for the bereft but not their home.

151

Money in the family, which helps some to behave calmly and adds tone, I do not have.

Nor is purchase of property part of my repertoire.

And your 'patient suffering world' is a pure coefficient.

Not of course that I am 'Benefits Street' or worse; far from it.

The bells of redeemed Rhymney a reclaimed harmony, a legend, a re-reading, a rhyming game.

....

In each particle the quantum bleeds us to a phantom, your poltergeist is real; a dust-mote's cosmos looks good on photos.

The true commonweal is as you feel; and as things lie without commentary. Numbers prevail:

Ideal 'Bryngwyn' evanescent from the renascent Welsh literary scene.

THE BOOK OF BARUCH BY THE GNOSTIC JUSTIN

152

The common thing to say about Alun is that he was accident-prone. I have
already done so. But it is true. An innocent game of improvised soccer with
his men would see him cased in plaster down at the base hospital in Poona.
He was, according to the common jester, a disaster waiting to happen.

That he should shoot himself—alas, not in the foot—en route to the latrines,
would be fully in keeping with earlier tragicomic scenes.

As others have said previously he lived directly not deviously. But he was a
good poet—with one great poem to his name—and thereby probably
ex officio fated.

The living grame of many an unthriving ex-officer of that time would not be
his to endure.

'Song (on seeing dead bodies floating off the Cape)' is sublime in its wanhope.

And his 'robustness in the core of sadness' rejoices even as it saddens.

153

The earth's curve leaves you at some further removes from her: strange it is
not unfamiliar.

Incur tenuous one-way dialogue: 'Two horsemen with a dog carved in red stone'.

There is yet question whether love would survive the cobra of grief; or the poet
his stint as tomb-robber to the life.

Re-edification of the Irish coinage, when the republic was in its nonage, dealt
grandly with the stranded sob story, transcended even the best statue—
Cuchulain's in situ—the Post Office as place both of business and rite—
gave Eire her European status and Pisistratan designs.

Our prejudices and cunning set the juices running.

154

Cinquefoil apple-flowers touch down in grass; early roses crouch to rawer ses-
sions; irises appear painted on glass. All are powers.

Wind's light glissando through the green strands so well defined: as to the
celestial mind in its rotunda, its panopticon:

So that I am inclined to say, leave well alone.

The utterly dire disciples are on their way, and have no shame. Nor do they tire
latterly despite the distances they have to come:

While a mild-seeming muddled worker bee mistakenly disburdens her swollen
legs of pollen, wringing herself dry on my knee.

155

As one or other has effectively said, resurrected is not exactly revived.
Define and yet again define wears definition to ruin.
Touch my lips and tongue with a live coal, I will not sing but recoil, as anyone
    would, not pre-selected by God, anathema riproaring among cosmic
    blips: a plethora of themes.
In fact *speechless infant* does not appear anywhere in the New Testament. Why
    did I ever suppose that it is there between Christmas and the New Year?
Poem as some kind of autonomous claim, the nominative of profound, and at
    a rate of late over-excitement about prime command.
Let me recall us to our ancient satiro-critical vein if we can still bear sovereign life.
Or, turning things over, be clever but benign in warning.

156

The ordeal of shaping fantasy that does not betray the real is confusing in
    More's parable of the isolate commonweal, as in all Tudor treatises on
    public order, one might add.
It is not, given these authors, the spheres of congruence but the sense of galled
    withers that pyrrhic Wyatt, who 'thinks as he grieves', perceives and
    pauses over in the telling guise of a lover.
Imminent self-containment of admired gab, scared genius of the furred robe,
    his mien not precisely that depicted by Hans Holbein, I would hazard.
'Christ is no wild-cat' says a preacher; but later; his words like a clawed spat on
    the tiles.
Confer for such matter 'the Word of God became a babe that cried'—Justin
    Martyr.
I have no desire to meditate on any state you might host me in; though 'Christ
    is no wild-cat' got to inspire Eliot I am not his sort of spoiled priest.

157

Held together by non-metals like oxygen the transparent motels.
To the epic theatre General Lucullus is not Werther.
To the epic theatre, which must be museless, Werther's sorrows are useless.
A wise saying by a man who overheard Confucius playing.
There will be somewhere a Chinese written character for this.
To the epic theatre General Lucullus is part of the eternal parities.
A wise woman in the ruins of a city is one of life's priorities.
To the epic theatre General Lucullus is not merely an absurd topic of regardful
    pride. He would go well in a Confucian ode.
Here is the preamble to my ancient ambition. It has taken the unwaged time
    of the nation to assemble and should be encouraged.

158

Ceremonies and music are the emotions of the universe is another ripe one. If it is
    not wholly forgotten why should I repine?
Who or what is *the Officer standing over the Heart*? Other, that is, than fidelity
    of report, the soul's status.
If not log of civilian photographer in war zone or town with plague.
From that Land of the Two Rivers good Lord deliver us. Forgive the promis-
    cuity of my Muse.
To the epic theatre General Lucullus's stature equals that of a cherry tree, its
    slightest feature his finest venture.
Poem as a form of amber rheum. Time the echo-chamber.
In the epic theatre we must attend while General Lucullus's end is determined
    by the base unservile class.
Status, posture, are undermined, though not those of the epic theatre which
    appears about to rehearse its yellow-highlighted and underlined future.
Despite what you say I trust Chou En-Lai; he has a good face. That is not the
    case with many whom the West fears.
The nearest we get to epic theatre is *The Orators*.
I dispute that; I am a student of *The Cantos* and of stately irate Yeats.
But it's a relief not to have to invent candidates.

159

Well into late May the lime leaves, to my inexpert eye, seem able to interrelate
    with light as in pure fable.
And the early roses now sway more weightily in the gardens of the new houses.
The apple blossom and the hawthorn blossom are gone. There remains a broad
    variousness of matt and gloss green.
Dead fledgelings are tossed by custom onto the compost.
There is colloquy, even at noonday, between us and our neighbour Venus.

160

Swags of rubberized gasbags lined with gold-beater's skin, obsolete from
    inception, overstressed, left out in the rain, too large for the garbage: the
    flailing ghosts of Cardington again.
It is closed season for ever in the Qattara Depression that saved the Eighth
    Army now so shaky, old-chummy and out of cover.
The 'fast convoys' to Malta cast images on time's retina: the tanker 'Ohio',
    her scorched, gashed, mute introit, lashed to destroyers to remain afloat,
    majestic in her slow distress, bearing down to her station with final
    deliberation and unquenched dark coronal.
Pay me my retainer. 'Untouched and in control' I shall labour to tell all.

161

Had I been out alone at night I would have crossed the street so as not to meet
    the young Bert Brecht.
Things would have been the same had I spotted T. E. Hulme in good time.
Both dead, I read and admire so dissimilar a pair.
General Lucullus could have proved hard to avoid.
Punch override. Reclue the thread.
Though another Lucullus is unlikely to rule us.
We rebecome citizenry, they say, when we experience life-changing chronic
    pain and/or begin using a Zimmer frame: triage our one remaining
    democratic privilege.
Egalitarian is what they mean; but that has not been English since I was a
    youngish man; and wasn't *echt* even then.
Things are indeed hapless. Nonetheless there are worse rulers, and peoples in
    greater need than us: as Bert Brecht, among many, could have given
    sworn testimony on; and in one mode did, with his epic theatre.

162

'The revolution of melancholick blood, which throweth up fastidious fumes
into the head' is a ready-made rhyme-scoop.
This is a vein in which Wotton and I have always got on; yet of the two he was
the more put upon.
I have never needed to plead for my salary; though it would have been in my
best interest to write as charily as he did.
Typical of his time: it was something flippant, an erudite Latin joke un-Latined,
that nearly broke him, wasn't it?
That is unlikely to be my lot.
His verses to the Winter Queen held neatly aloof from the internecine strife of
her brief reign; with too much of the 'Aethiops Eare' in their metaphor; but
sweetly penned. He was a practised schemer in the business of Bohemia.
Like picklocks and other devices verses served his purposing mind.

163

How much erudition the nation can tolerate has not, since Milton and Swift,
been a question even on the margin of state.
I no longer care that this protest is not syntactically neat.
'Who can discern those planets that are oft combust . . .', *ad infinitum*.
These are steady, in their own way, on their inveterate orbits around the Sun's
great girth, as is the Earth, even when Ptolemy holds sway.
That the young Milton met old Galileo we know on the strong authority of
Areopagitica.
Panta rhei: once again all things begin to flow; though *with no injury done to
hierarchy*, I believe Milton would have found it necessary to add, with or
without the accessory of rhyme.
There will be many who advise scepticism, mockery even. Poem as inaccurate
prism inaccurately decoded; progressively derided; making honest
decent people appear stupid; all the pretence of a séance; something
righteously to resent.
But hierarchy is not peerage-hegemony or the squirearchy, as at a time when
many must beg.
Intrinsic value is not even that strange coin of seventeen ninety-seven.
Intrinsic value that I care about is as tenuous and wiry as a bit of great verse.
Wood's well-nigh-implanted ha'pence, minted in brass or some such base
metal, found Swift's wit in high fettle; for whom let already guaranteed
praise be currently re-assayed and extravagantly spread.

164

Let's pretend that we demand recognition rather than spooked emotion
    at a tragedy's end. It is to my mind like Brecht's 'estrangement'
    (or 'alienation'); like being under newly revoked management.

The gift for metaphor is one of the poet's greatest assets: so said the
    Philosopher; though there is then a rift; or he stops short of what I could
    have him declare.

Or, put it this way: I would demote simile as being to poetry what calamine is
    for lotion or camomile for tea.

'Plato banished poets out of his Republique' in one of his fits of politic pique.

Aristotle does not lapse into such twaddle and tattle, one hopes.

I will give you my password to such eloquence as seldom before was heard.

Poisoned at a Symposium I seem to recall on someone's tomb. But where and
    of whom?

165

The subterrane genius of Newton is a portion of gravity, but not heinous, with
    nothing (or very little) that inclines to depravity—except in the sense
    that Jonathan Edwards (who, I believe, read him) could weigh well the
    pondus of the fallen world; the tragic inevitability of the Fall.

Newton did interpolate, amid memoranda of weight, trivia of domestic need;
    what to send the maid out to get from this or that street vendor. And
    boghouse was a word of widespread common use; it was where you
    stooped for a shit—obviously the rhyme words need to fall pat.

His question may incline a smidgen towards paranoia; and he may have been
    an odd curmudgeon. He had gnostic and iconoclastic leanings; though
    nothing too drastic and no harm done.

The radio telescope has recently bent his beauty out of shape; more than it has
    damaged—say—Palladio. This is not an occasion for that pity which is
    so much in fashion (can't stop to explain—have to run—but, my word
    on it, Hon, it's alright).

166

Spry young Berkeley, remarkably, decided that *particles* are units in the mind's
    energy; and thereby invented modernist poetry, as if for a bet. Yeats
    gives him credit for the magical feat but postmodernists denigrate it.

Opticks made feasible like invisible rope-tricks...

Ideal intellectual boy replaced by moony-faced Ordinary of Cloyne—too soon,
    I feel; but I may be unreal.

The third dimension is Imagination's apprehension (as Berkeley saw it; and
    Bomberg drew it). Whatever that means, I do glimpse it when little else
    intervenes.

The eternal verities are to vanish like fully disposed-of impurities?

167

That Rimbaud had read Berkeley is altogether unlikely. I can't see why, though
    able, he would bother; he already knows it all. See *A Season in Hell*,
    obviously.

Slack fluency and stark abruption are now our double portion and spell
    trouble.

The carnal drôle from Charleville could entertain particles of the mind's
    obscene energy even before he was born.

It is never too soon to learn that; if to be a poet is set into your pre-natal nerve
    pattern, as in his case it was.

Odd creature of mature fabulous inquiry, he will be free to retire soon, at
    twenty or twenty-one, with his untranslatable good fortune that seems
    certain not to bode at all well.

168

Putrescent idol of retail present in rich detail. Who said art is not entrepre-
    neurial? It is that or it is down and out. Mostly not the latter. Things are
    looking a shade brighter in the house of the distressed poetaster.

Shedding of semen within and without the womb. Nose near the orifice of
    shame; tongue in grime. Of some use to the concept of divine poem this
    Tertullian-like wedding hymn.

Noli me tangere made to sound oily and prim when, in the context of due time,
    a move crucial to the game of mystical love.

I pluck and suck my way to the heart of the artichoke.

169

I would versify, if I could, *The Art of Being Ruled*. I do paraphrase his perverse
   genius; he is not one of us, Percy Wyndham Lewis; but, prescient on our
   behalf, foresaw the selfie, the sicky gloss of candy-floss devoured without
   retching; one's own asinine preaching from stock. I

Doubt that Brecht would have dissed the methodism of a 'seditious Jesuit' had
   he known it to exist; though the mission to England fell into misprision
   and ended badly, except for the curious precision of their style, both
   prose and verse.

Lewis was like Nashe; whom he thought brash. Both men understood the
   overweening spite of the public word in the domain of fraud; the impo-
   tence of private truth sliding into mere credence-sloth.

Much good may they do us—the repetitious scorn of Percy Wyndham Lewis;
   the great writer who was Tom Nashe unearthed from an old crock or
   câche, or perhaps a plague-pit, more than a century ago; and put together
   with the best scholarly glue, reviving his set-to with pert Marprelate; his
   finest poem thrown away on a dull drama because it will do to meet the
   exigencies of what moves us to shamed stammer.

170

Muse-struck, stuck between chalk and fen where stump willows grow in a rag-
   ged line, is where this work has arisen while the rest of me has accus-
   tomed itself to the new horizon, still doing what I have always done best.

Is the old bent man entering the stone door by consent of his own scant
   wretched volition, notwithstanding Blake's willing that motion? I pre-
   tend a strong vision of wind in the skyscape and landscape behind, that
   I have also largely imagined.

His forehead projects a fierce quiff, the stiff final memento of his seminal life;
   his beard imitates mine in my mock senile portraits; the hem of his
   sackcloth robe agitates on the obscured path of ancient enforced sloth.
   It seems 'vexed' like the attire of a leechgatherer or some other slow
   hither-and-thitherer.

But that is not Blake's theme in his rhapsodic poem, where moribund auto-
   cracy has stayed too long this side the tomb. The old lad could even be
   George the Third withdrawing from Massachusetts' sanguine rim with
   umbrage to his name.

America is an early radiant work if we simply let the illumination bathe us.

So Blake has come within an ace of begetting Los with not the least tincture of
   natural human shame and without bathos.

171

Land's End and back in a day: not something I would recommend, especially if you are a retiree and live in East Anglia.

Frequently, since, I have retransmitted my soul on its remote frequency to squatting Cornwall: half-wasted sub-tropical; few signs of camelottage except for a distant sighting of St Michael's Mount sunlit but eerie, of no set age.

Moving in history as in a strange convention with its own timing, rhyme scheme and scansion; destiny the anagram of a fated name, of which I surrender the difficulty to another faculty—it is not a crime. Though grammar has grown arbitrary she is stuck with my oratory and is—*ad absurdum*—its theme.

Should I not have wired you earlier? Would things have appeared less peculiar than I had feared?

Examine me, you who shall lovers be, chameleon with slow reflex, not catching up with a fix of new colour in time to save my skin.

I shall never now be guided where famed Goonamarris glares its lopsided eye of clay.

Not that I feel it likely I would be unwelcomed there or shamed by the deaf-blind man's acclaimed poetry.

172

There is a distinct Irish tradition of comic erudition which is greatly to the credit of that nation.

Tom Sheridan's cod-Latin letter to Dean Swift could be read by mistake as something dropped from *Finnegans Wake*, or so I should have hoped.

'The autonomy of the pony' is an imperfect rhyme though it helped make the name of Myles na Gopaleen.

Do the women still cry 'free Brian Toy' outside the wall at Mountjoy Gaol?

Call that funny? Back to your cell.

Know the enemy. Poem as self-administered castor oil enema.

173

Most members of the police were renegade working class. In my childhood, that was.

At Fairfield I felt it scald where I was first schooled in class-climbing, coward-ice and the art of rhyming.

Nouns, especially nouns of propriety, exude malign pheromones. Cast them back in the sea, among the hearty sea-bass runs.

Vacant Rimbaud imbibed squid ink and shark sperm and went deep to do so. Unlike Crusoe.

Now in his self-coherent self-damnation as happy as a sandboy; vice-gerent of Ethiopia, inventor of the photocopier and mechanical croupier.

There is some kind of imbalance here between history and hysteria.

It can't be excess testosterone; I have none, lady in the white dress!

174

'All the mirrors in England are broken' I've taken from *Jonathan Strange & Mr Norrell*. Possibly it is how we all feel.

Nothing here remains obscure. But there are many crossed wires, even as wires become archaic metaphors.

'The conversation of mankind' is politically condoned. But things are not like that on the estate, in the *état*, wherever.

Mediocrity in the seventeenth-century political fable meant on the whole something admirable.

Enthusiasm was a malign spasm in faith or polity and ran to trouble.

But that was then. I would not have known how to hold a pen.

The canon is a chain letter to which you must commit; there is a curse on it like a cast rune.

To come up with a good line is like briefly discovering that you are sane.

What survives of spirit is method; or method withstood; which indeed has the greater merit.

175

'The human condition' is interviewed for yet another menial situation in a tone appropriate to *The Moonstone*, *Lady Audley's Secret*, or *A Good Read*.

You asked my opinion of the great in their mood, Mr Toad.

This is the edge of Sandringham country and I am not at home.

The Chinese, with inventive finesse, call a full moon the 'ice wheel'.

The road leading north is crystallized in its own breath.

The re-edification of the nation—England to be precise—is a done deal.

'Good old dream, how handy you are', hear friend Wyndham exclaim and declare, some four years on from *Childermass*-time, when I am not quite ready to enter the womb; when I cannot possess even an embryo skull to bless and wax symbolic over and possibly exorcise with the kiss of wit, my lover.

'The dregs of the people alone survive to witness'—saving only the priest who I suppose wrote this: at Ashwell 'on the borders of the Cambridgeshire levels' when England was the plague's and, some undoubtedly would have believed, the devil's.

Active and passive resentment squabble at the top of my ugly mental slide in the yard of a village school.

The celebrated fields of arable, long deliberated by those who have planned wisely the entertainment of their land, retain, even now, a long absorbent glow, of the kind that elsewhere only triumphal self-righteousness can show.

176

How do I think I rate? Just about on a par with Nahum Tate whose word-book
for *Dido and Aeneas* is rightly admired, albeit by few.

Mainchance the same now as then: a sow on her side in the muck-mushy straw
like a female pasha, her grand rootling progeny never quite sucking her dry.

'The Blessed Virgin's Expostulation' Tate also gave (or sold) Purcell to
refashion, which he did, turning prim couplets into sprung rhythm
two centuries before 'That Nature is a Heraclitean fire' which its
rediscoverer—a devout Purcell admirer—felt duty bound to keep
hidden lest he should bring notoriety upon the Society in which you do
as you are bidden.

Nahum became, in the flatness of celebrity time, 'king's canary' to William and
Mary. It was a jobber's wreath and suited him. Though he was mocked
for it his availability can be seen not to have lacked worth.

The occasional royal hand is extended to poetry still, perhaps because other-
wise it is so unmemorable. Certainly the Queen has not remembered it
in her will.

177

The *Childermass* bombardier I do my best to admire, though his tractate *Hitler*
was the worst headless chicken act of the literary thirties.

Worse than Henry Williamson, was he, then?

There were things held in common with all who angrily mourn and curse and
otherwise display distress.

They were a right pair of shell-shocked intellectual beauties, each with his
high manner of reproof that was also a moral boner.

Henry was a Jeremiah and, like him, bought a field in Anathoth (blessings be
upon them both for that); I did not.

Henry was the one ⎮ able there and then to move in to his prestigious but
penurious wone; to begin chasing the dragon's tail of prophetic cerebral
sin; who could not be confident of a rabbit on which to dine.

I use metaphor to be sure.

Das feste Rückgrat der Bewegung—'feste' gives it a spurious Lutheran twist—
was not worth having bloodied-up the wrong spoor.

In my case it is the prologue to the *First Dialogue* that nails me as one danger-
ously at ease with defeatist tales.

178

Conisbrough's light-concentrate gnomon that we catch sight of along the A1, as we do York, Ely or Durham from the train: these mark-points in the vigilance of England (Blighty being in thrall to an almighty spell contrived both by those who conform and those who rebel), the archaic switchboard gene that illuminates my brain whenever history is near: 'Geoff's Mystery Tour', perilous self-entertainment that would have delighted my Aunt Nell, the bright one of our family. If she were still here I would try to persuade her to recite *Wulfstan's Homily*, by heart, for pleasurable instruction, hers and mine, the ultimate fable of millennial reign.

179

'Man is the dwarf of himself', Mr Toad, as you have written in your inspired creed that is at least equal, if not superior, to Breton's 'Ode to Fourier', and the making of your career.

The poem as escapade does not do justice to the dadaist hobby horse ride. And Tzara is the crucial mock faddist without whom we cannot reduce the circle to the square.

Those 'chagrins which the bad heart gives off' I have known since my ninth birthday as the intestinal marsh gas of self-pity, a pathetic wraith of which a lit poem is the certifiably ideal blue flame.

What did you think it was that I had ventured upon not to say? That I would leave no time for reply to a question you had not heard correctly because it is in rhyme?

'We can know only what we ourselves have made.' But I am more Larkin *père* than I am Phil or Ted, Thom, Marvell, Emily, Apollinaire.

Ted also bought his field in Anathoth when fearful reason could well have advised staying put.

Not all enviable rewards are due to wire-pull: instance *Lupercal* even now applauded wildly up in the gods.

180

At Harrow on the Hill the harrowing of hell. Mr Jones is unwell.

The fact of death comes up on the unfelt birth of a breath.

Tell the Ancient Mariner to pipe down. We agree that he is a great sinner.
Let the guilds of Chester sign the memorial register.

Cottage garden hollyhocks that do not overreach, though Eliot in his
acting-up early dotage stooped to pretend so to preach, let us present as
to a long-service school-crossing warden on her retirement.

Fox faeces and lavender in a beribboned box return to sender.

Gloriana—at her exequies Shakespeare could have been a senior mourner.
Was he?

Impossible to know, between now and tomorrow, what they see in us or how
powerful their throw.

As most by now are aware, Britain has no winding gear any more:

Justice, injustice, wait to be reclaimed in a renamed vacant square.

Despite cant-caveat—know what I mean, eh?—latterday Labour a malign
chant one can't mourn.

Poem as prime site. Poem as a slime *in situ*.

181

Repetitiousness stems from ignorance and distress; probably not both at once.

Scansion is repetition in pattern; and an enduring mansion.

Meanwhile, be not idle with what remains of time.

Pre-extremis, one may deliver decorum of theme, even with a prostate biopsy-
needle stuck up your taut rectum.

For example, a tall calm poem from the Temple of Ancient Virtue in the gar-
dens at Stowe.

Truth's ever self-evident grandeur let us ascribe to Pindar who is currently in:

Though he could play rough with the prescribed play-dough of public
encomium

Which is always a good sign whether or not the urine specimen is mine.

182

At which point I encountered by rogue chance in a Cecil Court catalogue
  Lichtenberg's *Commentaries on Hogarth* and did yet another *ad hoc* intel-
  ligence dance for the improving centuries and the merchant venturers of
  art. Hence,

Hogarth and Lichtenberg, both: I offer them jointly a serrated wreath while
  England staggers about the heath arointly and I hold vigil for art and
  hierarchy, and league and blind segue.

Morning: London's griped *in situ*, frozen-piped, shallow-pilastered brick of
  speculation, brinksman-bank-barrack pile or stack, by unseen sun and
  moon, each exorbitant tenant; snow brewed from builders' dirt and
  soot and mutant rain. Iron sheathing of pattens and patents; portents;
  starvelings and slatterns; the spit-proud old maid, church-recking, her
  attitude of bitten-back tirade; all crueller than first day in a great school-
  yard or a Newgate birthing. Dread and loathing by brute rote overfed,
  fattened for the Lord Mayor's table where the civic odes are execrable.

There is something in the static surges of *Morning* that purges witness, exposes
  moral purpose as gross importuning; subject of course to Hogarth's rig-
  ours of persuasiveness.

'A world exhilarating and wrong', that equation wrenched from striation, must
  belong to some parallel alien routine of celebratory song.

'The One, the Few, the Many': where does Swift draft or imply this austere
  hierarchy that opens like a painted fan upon tainted air?

In *A Midnight Modern Conversation*, the benevolent clergy person presides
  without curate but with a putto or two, round table argle-bargle; an
  invisible parrot. Curtailment of noon-style sway of reason (it appears to
  be draped day) around the beneficent bowl, tun or urn and the parson's
  exemplary item of a spoon.

This could become a burden to him but evidently not soon. He will get back to
  Tillotson in good time.

Meanwhile it is a charade none can ride without grasping the tail of the mule.

Lichtenberg has a phrase for it, I can't rightly recall: *acting in the wrong time?*
  The clock convinces us with its identifying chime that reason is both
  short and long division; to which we are answerable like good children at
  table; and that reality is indivisible—

Whereas in fact our tipsy lucubrations swell and contract, drunk on tasteless
  contumely; incapable of the sum of the nations as with any Augustan
  disequilibrium of taste and tact.

In Hogarth the clocks make faces at us. No-one is quite sure why this is so, despite numerous theories and rote inquiries.

I repeat: we are shown a domain in which equability is a rare feat and where time is a solipsism (to some ways of thinking).

With Lichtenberg profundity was a form of blague or perhaps a hair of the dog. Avoid the radio epilogue and the art of sinking.

Before dug-in Meridian, that near-inaudible monologue of the Sun suited everyone and none. Before steam's rigadon-organ the pardon might reach and touch out of time's unconsidered pleach to considerable acclaim.

Time could be grim. But, as Marvell protested, one might give it a run and fancy us unbested.

I care little for the Lockean power that has botched metaphor and straitened the hour; but my reasoning is poor.

Look again at the barrack-block houses in Hogarth's *Morning*; hear the noises of the clocks running in their well-set cases, even though propulsive steam is not yet entirely in harness.

. . . .

A mere shattering of China dinner plates is not even one of *Marriage à la Mode*'s minor episodes.

In Augustan art the malign is only part-done when the curtain comes down. Hogarth's engravures are staffed by false saviours, the survivors.

I cannot discard this card or this cur from the pack of *Morning* though I might wish I could, Dr Arbuthnot, sir: you see how it preys on my mind with a reek of burning and some kind of unheard sound.

Destinies incorporate with laziness and vicious entreprise are unlaced here.

A Harlot's Progress: a word to the wise. The poor curate's dim, harmless daughter is pimped *non pro rata* by a rich hag while—look at him!—he sits a yard off, cramped in the saddle of a blown nag cheated of its nose-bag.

Even the great engraver seems culpable: complicit spiv to prurient curiosity his client.

But like most artists he is an accomplished self-forgiver.

. . . .

Property, propriety, and poetic authority: these three are everywhere in eighteenth-century satire.

Defuse and discuss; that is what discussion means in these neo-Laputan academies. *Sunbeams out of cucumbers.*

The banished racket of oak and oik too much like Newmarket?

Yet horses are among our members.

Mooncalf, I barely but half-know what I am about. I am the black boy in the turban, morning hot chocolate my satirical burden. Agh, don't be absurd!

Drin-dran, *drin-dran*, the drums.

Not all impromptus are tantrums.

It was no primitive intelligence that could conceive of bronze. And that was aeons before these feckless ones changed the scenes, and politeness became deranged and an entrée to hell's pantry; and moral genius was sent to Coventry, i.e., Twickenham, Dublin.

There is no quarrel between us though double the pain.

....

The Sun is held in suspense between force of gravity and pace of nuclear fusion.

The England of my fable an unstable floating island seldom in the same place: ideal Tudor fool-trial or draggled tape-loop found among effects of the late Mr Pope; or Hogarth—his take on brides in the bath.

Not my prime purpose of jollity to lecture our all-expenses-paid nobility on mobility and fixture. I turn my laugh to the wall though not at all for privacy or charity.

Terrible journey's claim to become inheritable sojourn. For some it does. How ambiguous the starkest grame-idiom of Brit poem-frame as the main feature.

I write for full-gut instrument from seventeen thirty-eight or thereabout, probably of London style, fret, and sleight.

The form I choose is monologue though with frequent episodes of multi-voiced fugue.

Whoever served as model for the man at the harpsichord in scene two of *The Rake's Progress* it is unlikely to have been Handel, though many so sneered at the time, no doubt to cause him distress with a smear of scandal and scurrilous rhyme.

Nothing new to me that for self-loathing you now desire to rip your section from the directory, then swallow fire. But such instances are rare.

Poem as bold pioneering type of spinal tap into nature; in the hands of an amateur liable to fatal mishap.

....

To be made to pay for being in debtors' prison: it is becoming like that again
    in the rank starveling season of unconstrained foetors. We stand looking
    in at ourselves, marvelling, as though at a fresh Hogarth engraving.
To keep faith in an England that processes worth is like still believing in a
    flat earth.
'England' must stand for the entire nation in this type of antique protestation,
    as it could have been heard during the Restoration, that dire Assyriad
    and moral Babel where Bunyan wilfully refloated the unwieldy Bible
    unaided; or at the period of the Bubble.
'Nails must be driven in point first.' Even this now strains trust. Impossible to
    hammer the phantoms of past clamour or to nail the dust.
Hogarth still stares down at us magisterially priced.
The daemon of commodity techne is, and ever was, daemonic Arachne for
    whom many at one go become a quick snack.

183

Who knows what another feels, especially about industrials? Investment with-
    out industry a new version of strength through joy.
Liverpool's façade of culture, a half mile thick at most; after which it is still
    thin brick, soot crust; and a Catholicism of sepulture and cost.
The administration of intestate goods by a glutted nation that passes on fate.
'With Hegel the object vanishes into the dialectal process.'
Magnificent moon-wrought surface of ocean; and a taught life of service.
The Crystal Palace ablaze, cascading-in upon itself like crazy.
All the *mysterium* of God is in the measure of time.

184

The atrocious power of great bad art—things like the Nibelungs—inspires the
  facetious. That insight is probably Nietzsche's.
Foch too was prescient, 'an armistice of twenty years'. He should have been
  President.
Cigarette after coitus: rhetorical proclivities perhaps equal to two semibreves.
Throwaway right to the heart: Bacall and Bogart; *Love's Martyr*.
Some can create from a disparity that would silence someone better.
Did poorest Jews have to purchase the worst names? The Mandelstams, then,
  must have pawned a few gems. File under *apocryphal*.
The welting candles that bloat as they strip and float in a kind of miniature
  skip mismeasure prayers' sinecures.
'Sharp and pregnant wit' we will not get in the present context, even with due
  benefit of doubt.
Vexed, Alice has pashed through a lake of tears and rabbits' piss for a vindica-
  tion of decorous habits.
Versailles to Vichy: the déjà-vu cliché that is true.

185

Upcoming death, bestir the 'opposite motion' of my 'orb', bringing it
  'against'—as they said then—the Sun, there to outshine some others in
  the competitive spin of our envious throes carousing.
Purcell's *Odes and Welcome Songs* set me brooding on my wrongs, which was
  not their commission and which must stand for my confession, I suppose.
But this is where one rightly belongs, nonetheless; with the intrepid, noble-
  spritely Muse, with yourself as obtuse, with mere invention as a stint of
  well-nigh infinite redress.

....

In Purcell's time it was John Aubrey fiddling at Avebury.
And still the large flint axes come up from the damp deep clamps.

186

This, it is becoming clear, is more a daybook than ever *The Daybooks* were:
il mestiere di vivere that secures its own private consistory and guards the
door, admitting neither rich nor poor to the designs and details of poetry
which are the very devil to portray without favour or fear.

Corbyn must win. Though he is a flawed man it is not my belief that Hogarth
would set him down as a tout or a thief.

To ask whether Labour could ever again take power is beside the point at this
juncture and hour.

Let me recommence my old caterwaul of 'intrinsic value', if only to rile you.

But why should you be riled at all? No disordinancy has been revealed, other
than in the cabals that have reviled Corbyn with claptrap lobbymen.

It is the lobby that corrupts the language of praise, determines greatness to be
derisory. I should not trust even Hogarth on the topic of Jews and usury.
And Cobbett would be worse. I count them among my grievous heroes,
whose structural stature—each minúte particular of unbribed observa-
tion, whether of turnip or fashion—combines in a singular authentic
judgement upon the nation.

187

'Celebrate this Festival (Birthday Ode for Queen Mary)', sixteen ninety-three.
With twenty-three more in all. There's a boxed set for sale on ebay.
Action this day. Fool!

A nice sociopathology at call: not democracy, then, but oligarchic mob rule,
suitable for portrayal by pre- and post-Hogarthian humorists, as we see
in a tidy Martin Rowson cartoon for the *Guardian*.

That it is all an inevitable consequence of the Fall we scarcely need Milton to
foretell or recall; nor indeed Dryden, late uncompromised apologist for
the previous reign who, a-twist in the silvery mucilage of the stage, yet
singularly failed to renege; lost his laureate status. This and suchlike
tragicomic sawdust afflatus.

Bussed-in democracy so dear to the inarticulate heart of the BBC Trust:
whether this henceforwardly will be part of the lost past is hardly for me
to say. What would Hogarth or Cobbett have said or thought? With what
mass opinion is Corbyn freighted but not fraught; as by garrulous Susan
of the parlous, inutile Horrabin line at Pebble Mill?

188

Sixteen ninety-three: it is getting late; for Purcell, certainly; and even more so
    for the 'noble and amiable' consort of the dourly alien head of state.

I am ready to be flexible, as you are: such immortality is correlatively fixable
    though relatively rare.

I shall vouch for you, Mary: you have done your stint as Protestant Nationalist
    Saint.

And these 'welcome songs' feature a benign vision for the future of the
    kingdom in accordance with divine nature.

Let's dance.

'Yet fears advance.'

Strung-along Purcell's England was in many ways fit to be hanged. His music
    ('wondrous machine'), though surely more than a gnostic bathysphere
    that could sustain immense pressure, was that nonetheless.

These patterns, here, of internal rhyme are set to do more than mnemonically
    chime.

They form the DNA of a lay, a poem that I intend shall comprehend the mind
    and clay of some sane realm.

In sixteen ninety-three, as now, what did *sane* mean, other than rightly-constituted
    energy? Or sixteen ninety-four, just to be sure.

189

Ich bin Dreyfus, an old man who walks with a cane, thus—

That simple riddle of the Sphinx which prevailed to jinx the ancient world—

Shaking all over I am soon to discover the Cave of Unmaking: to my inexact
    knowledge probably a Blake thing. I shall not act nobly.

Ah, Purcell, sublimely professional: able to change single- to multi-syllable
    rhymes; who in the mind's labyrinth can find and follow the theme's
    clue to whatever length, silently utters the pitch of virtuoso trumpeters
    and canonic sopranos; nothing unsingsingsingable. Tell him his saddest
    music well-betides us, elides all but our last, worst fears.

He knows; but tell him anyway; caught as he is in eulogies and elegies, he may
    catch what you say.

But spare him my treatise on music and gnostic poiesis.

190

Worst scenario could be comic; to believe otherwise would be to presume on
    some slewed pseudo-Calvinist creed.

The humours, an outmanoeuvred crux of psychosis, even now bode crises.

Time not truly a furious eye? I'm at a loss to try if that is so.

Call the incurious the true Furies?

....

Lack of machine logic may be a redemptive magic, albeit far from strategic.

'Duke of dark corners', old *drôle-de-drame*, emerge from your cordon of
    treacherous mourners, become belated late patron of my poem.

Cannabis inhaled by vatic wannabes, that smelt like stale female underarm
    sweat in a squat, is not what it was.

Crystal meth frees us from hearth and home. 'To the Memory of An
    Unfortunate Lady' would use up too much space on the tomb.

Sincerity is, finally, an unparticular old fright. That this is dumb mouthing in
    spite, my ape an uptight convert rigorist in pen and penis, grows evident
    from the mise-en-scène, like that Tudor codpiece, like an old man's dojo;
    the cold greed of Angelo who was not old.

Perhaps I should read sad Berryman again. The scheme of this poem did not
    come to my head like the Twelve Step Programme in an alternative
    form.

Most times, in the matter of poems, I follow where I lead.

....

Media no true medium. If unrepentant now, then in any new time?

Corbyn's win. Democracy sprung, new-old blood, from stock and stone.
    Tribute to, yet break from, the great dead and my dead kin.

Britain otherwise unstrung, a-swim with demos; woe to Demos.

Fatal heart attack, from now on, for a whack, an existential and a political mis-
    take. Check-in quick for vital check-up.

'Party grandees', the phrase chimes always with rote applause, some sleaze.

Must admit, favoured dodgy epilogue not now or ever hugely in vogue.

O language, my allergy, my bloody colleague!

191

Hard birthings and cold hearths. And deaths and earthings. Marriage as a malign spell.

She writes well of people who are near-mutes; imitates Andersen and a Russian folk tale: the stranger with whom I exchanged a one-off kiss and from whom, after six decades, transpose and reprise the words I italicize; who 'sadly' entered the tomb, as we say of those who succumb before full time; but with a good legacy and with a fair measure of praise.

In extremis will take speech from us, even the famous. It is a dire *traum* that moves towards the grotesque theatre of a medieval Doom; or not, according to some cankered whim of nature.

You can shed black blood or black bile if you like; if you think these contain your mood and your style.

Rage does not self-assuage through the seepage of old age. Forgive the obviousness of the reminder, you, true and tender. I would avoid *lento*.

Irrelevance has its significances now, its odds and evens.

Art's aim is to scheme for a tight fit even so.

192

It is amazing, what we do to ourselves; and not by halves and not by mute navel-gazing.

Geoff is the here-subscribed, with the double stent and the naff haemorrhoid. Not a Kentish man nor a man of Kent, unlike Jack Cade or the younger Wyatt or Henry Wotton.

Though 'you may track him in their snow' is not mere pi-jaw; and gives me a broad constituency of staidness and frenzy: poetics, I concede, is indeed a lost cause to vote on; the original has become the marginal; melancholy is unruly.

Bringing riot to order: not exclusively Tudor. Ritual of commonweal possessed of sacred appeal; while verst beyond verst remained waste folk-heathland and royal forest.

Praxis took *dare: durst* for its axis; the best and the worst. Taxes made their own issue, of claimant and mayhem.

Corbyn would have gone to the stake or the Tyburn chopping-block, as soon as speak or look; a Kett-like protestor or some make of Anabaptist freak.

Don't laugh: an enigmatic point in a Tory tachygraph before the mid-century? Geoff would have applauded the contrary.

193

After those careers in the bloody exclusive wars, the Commonwealth stayed
with us four years, the Protectorate seven. Naseby was not the broad
straight swatheway to earthly heaven, as it had appeared when smoke
first cleared from the field.

Lilburne was soon gone; Hampden so early killed. Fairfax, no longer Fate's
artifex, withdrew to Nun Appleton. Vane, a toleration man, spread his
broad, unwise loyalties too thinly, some said. That did not save the skin
of his head. But you know these; and my numerous other sententious-
nesses over French fries.

Disaffection yet haled itself to, from, the New World, an uppity projection of
truth ejecting in a scrolled banner from its stiff mouth.

The oxymoron is a figure of frustration and grief; the paradox has shut down;
the grammar of salvation conceived for a language not now our own, if
Abdiel is still to be believed.

'For the vintage shall fail, the gathering shall not come' to them that had gath-
ered behind the drum.

I can't relate even the worst of these to our ignorant, ignoble premises of worth
and rate.

You must allow for my élitist hysterias, as people in the past were permitted
bomb stories.

194

Ignorance of the 'spiritual powers of darkness'—Winstanley. You need the
    right words plus the original wingspan of the angel to wrest this into
    your dizzily-promoted sacred *singspiel*.
Even then it may not happen, your long-desired eloquence, and well-shapen.
Complexities of the singular things rise against us, are multi-angular but not
    fixities.
Born to order, both extravagance and vagrancy.
One man's verses may be his pet form of wet psoriasis.
'Perhaps the unseemly is the part that survives'—Mrs Dalloway believes that
    she lately perceives calmly, prose-poemly, the diversity of occluded lives.
....

The making of a certain type of intricate *cursus* is read as a signal of political
    perverseness:
More so than a refusal even to mime that anthem—more properly the hymn—
    in the presence of ancient entranced veterans and HM.
High-functioning autism (Foot-ism) can create schism at the pull of a string.
    It happens in slow motion before the assembled nation. There was no
    rigor of intention. Anger is beside the point.
The radical politics are not an obstacle: a revival of archaic, anti-oligarchic zeal.
If the free spirit is unelectable, so be it.
Come the turn of the wheel it shall have my vote, posthumous or not.
....

Eighty's no time to revoke the djinn of pot-luck.
As the retroactive mind hovers between moves, the hypercritical may ask
    impossible favours from the receivers of tribute, *e.g.*
Poetry that—I confess—I won in the Lottery.
And you would like me to remain calm; not to have recourse again to the
    cursus; not to curse or recuse; but to re-imagine myself one of the slithily
    well-suited magi men.
Meanwhile we will continue to fawn on China rather than Taiwan.
Meanwhile abides also old Malc's *Ninth*, the belated final call that is interpret-
    able as granite-and-amaranth, if you will.
I trust he is bloody-minded—Corbyn—and in time will be well attended.
I must not imagine him the gnostic Justin.
An *all systems* warning seems unable to reach my tongue.

195

Grammar, the foundation of civic life, is now not even a pedantic gimmick, a
    Lego-like snapper-toy; and is brought into general contempt and goes
    incognito: she that was long sought by many lovers and true believers,
    yet no man's wife:

UR fired, being of Lord Sugar the grammatical signature, whom Chesterton
    would have dubbed oligarch, his befriending of New Labour notwith-
    standing; and who is pleased to be called ogre, with other dire words and
    phrases of remark:

The current Laureate, who invites us to celebrate an entire *Twitter*, as once
    she might have high-fived the *Tatler*, presents it as lead actor or agent in
    the democratic theatre (I use the word figuratively and concur with her
    that power should not be applied furtively). But brevity itself does not
    signal the nativity of a new openness, a new commonweal of agreeable
    opinions.

I am as much in love with the equitable as she is; but even so feel jilted and
    miserable; and sometimes tell myself lies:

Regarding creative freedom, its proclivities and tyrannical dominions.

196

The 'high dome of Paul's' these days appears to crouch, unless you approach
     from the direction of the Fleet ditch; which is in any case the way of
     tradition whose rites still confer benefits upon the nation.
The dry-mouthed state trumpeters contrive to spit a high pure note. The vault
     jitters at the impetus and, far below, something small immodestly clatters.
Cargo-cult majesty in Perrault travesty? Maybe, but not her fault.
The Lord Mayor's Show is a show of power that briefly throws the City out
     of gear.
A full state funeral is uncommon, nay, rare, whether for man or woman.
White youths who provoke riot declare themselves patriots, I dare say.
So, no doubt, did the younger Wyatt.
Pythagoras on music. The three : two ratio which is—'for all we know'—the
     comprehension of first creation; as Bull may have taught it well at
     Gresham College (that ninth *In Nomine* in a strange propulsive time) a
     virtuoso of occult knowledge considerably more precious than alchemy.
Sir Christopher Wren, in or around the year seventeen ten, *went to dine with
     some men*, memorially, with a view to re-edifying the clerihew.
How well he succeeded, if at all, is at present unclear. Nor is the gesture much
     noticed or applauded.
It is essential not to be goaded into a defiant posture.
Comedy is circumstantially providential; not exactly a remedy.

197

Old Malc: back in Northampton, the tragi-grotesque mask of rage clamped on.
Some shortcoming of the soul indelibly stamped: immoveable that snarl.
Perfidious the irritant solace of alcohol. I want! I want!
Symphony nine unwinds as though in unison on two staves, like a parody of
     Mahlerian benison.
Being ignorant of human physiology, surgery or medicine I would conclude
     the core of his brain gone, as with the snory noise of a shot man caught
     on the wire in that war memoir:
Which old Malc did not have to emit or hear or otherwise endure.
But, there! How it can haul itself from three craters in a row, that final untri-
     umphing *lento* of twenty-odd minutes, which mimes infinites without
     claims; can barely feel but persists in so rueing, though the wrists of the
     violinists must be wrung with the sustaining of its near subliminal song.

198

Shoeing of horses I recall well enough; the bellows handle up and doing with
　　its strong whuff. Hot iron on hoof horn; the shoe-nails hammered home
　　with foreshortened forearm strength—though I do not remember how
　　to shape this proto-Cubist photo for the epidiascope.

Or that snap of the chained Hereford bull on the pile of hay-bales; he appeared
　　terrifyingly mad though the breed as a rule is not so inclined to such
　　beastlihood.

At worst I take stock of a miniature flick-book, at which we would sneak a look
　　behind a raised desk lid as I have earlier described.

Arithmetic went click in the heads of the other kids. Some were set to do well:
　　took out patents; bought farms on which they had been tenants; who at
　　school sat in their own feral smell.

Poem as wrong key to the right kingdom.

199

Fugal music may sound skeletal, ludic yet regal; as in Purcell, Handel.

The body of England was mangled, plastered, clystered; good for nothing but
　　scat-pride, riot; loathing; loose-tongued yet curt, somewhat like John
　　Wilmot before his stop-press change of heart.

This endless name-dropping, with and without handles, is not—I repeat—my
　　form of coping with the nameless thing, our final and fatal lot.

Mere repetitiousness is not endurance; more a transference of oxymorons.

What I care most about, in the art I rate, is its strut: the toccata, in short.

200

Poem as the need to conform to some imagined power that could redeem a
　　near fatal solecism.

Simile is a dwarf homily; metaphor an intrinsic forensic power.

Truth is schism. Criticism a caucus plus a phantasm.

At most it is a serious business for the adept; and best kept from the idly
　　curious. Be my witness, will you, One-eyed Riley?

Poem as the extended possessive which may become massive and repossess
　　your home.

Poem as urgent sperm bank for sunk re-emergent nation is, I fear, mere
　　latterday swank.

201

Any time soon the rite of burial will be performed by drone. Baptism, for the
immediate future, will remain hands-on. Why?

I was myself briefly reputed, well before the middle years, to possess strange
powers: it is all available in the confidential bowers at Hereford-
Worcester. My earliest love is employed there as a de-ghoster.

Your true necromancer will always seek damages for harm done to reputation.
That is how you verify him or her. It is why I know for sure that I am
not one.

The middle echelon of a sacred institution, much like the constitution of a
secular state, confounds hierarchy with hegemony. Always has done.

Ecclesia Anglicana never really was the Marriage at Cana; though there were
ever too few able and willing to say why.

202

Trust the *geste* as you would an intelligent strength of wrist: what wise tradition
means by *spontaneous*; that keeps its distance from those inane *Guardian*
creatives and their patent mental laxatives.

The fatuous has vicious claws, and worse.

Enviably to say without bluster, 'I conceived this stanza while acting as beach-
master at Anzio. With luck and a quick polish you can demolish a Panzer;
though the Poles will always have the tactical edge which only fools
would grudge.'

There will be the occasional neo-Regency silly billy yet wily withal. The
immortal must be able to steal what it takes from the common gene-pool
without too many fakes that it likes too well.

Gnosticism's not schisms but norms, even when expressed in terms of theorems
and therms.

Poetry as revanchist oratory revanquished and revarnished. Key terms: fuga-
tory, mortuary, *unravished*, *wound-dresser*.

Poem as catarrhal fuel; as royal jelly in no way expecting such referral.

Plus other things into which one might read some of the beauties and advan-
tages of fugue: take time to re-rhyme; plan a dream epilogue.

Poem as adumbration of the Abbey of Thelema.

As slow-release semantic corm.

Poem as Bob's Thelma.

203

Three polite Americans parked under our fresh white horsechestnut tree to try their patience training homing pigeons. My mother made them tea. One bird would not 'home' after I had scared it by clapping at the wrong time.

I see myself as lost, even then, that child whom it would always be unwise to trust or to treat gently or to expect to act providently for others or for himself, a tyrannical waif of self-love.

Even now I would remove the period if I could, in my autocratically disposed mood.

204

Climb back into the desperate, stalled and fatuous time, as into a mission-ready, leaflet-laden Vickers Wellington or Bristol Blenheim.

Pathé uncouth throughout, voiced by the ubiquitous patriot-tout; thanks to whom Timoshenko, clockwork dummy of the Ukraine, became heroic in noisy British acclaim and student rhyme.

By curt disobedience, in nineteen forty Gort had saved our army in France.

To be all but cashiered was his reward. That he was spared I would attribute only in part to his being an Irish Lord.

Poem abandoned on the bridge of Arnhem with an understandable grudge against centuries of stultifying class privilege, even though those on the spot were good at dying.

Guilty of bad intelligence and intemperate tactics these were not. No-one of good faith could excuse GHQ's self-exculpating account of a transcendent stunt and an ultimately divine rating: the relief canisters haplessly gyrating, flubbing down, into enemy-secured sections of the law-abiding town.

205

Current condition of British poetry-nation much like that of semi-derelict
  Pitcairn or abandoned South American whaling station.

There is a stubborn clatter somewhere, as of a loose furnace-shutter.

From hyssop to gas tap: a mini-history of solipsistic verse. Mine? Hers?

Sooner or later a new accumulator for the moral motor seems in order; cheer-
  fully supplied by Joseph the Provider (*dein bruder*) for the good of all.

Poem as shark embryo; eats its kin in the womb.

Poem as my last authentic autistic chum. Verifiable by cable.

Verification by cable, even, too much trouble.

Poem as agent of Islam; headquarters alleged Chartres which is name and
  shame bound to host martyrs.

I have here a slim volume: my odes, largely made up of joking asides (*re* Bligh
  and Christian, Benjamin Britten). Wish British poetry once more prize
  thing of beauty.

On that note restore me your vote.

From Unity Mitford to *Barry Cryer at Eighty*: my epitome of Blighty, though
  not set in granite, may yet make Twitter fury sing a bit.

My Timon is not yet a total con-man. If you believe that so can I, and what
  fettle?

206

Christian faith a fraud? Question to turn on whether the Turin shroud is
  genuine?

Genuine, I imagine; having seen that electro-transference of dummy features
  to linen on screen.

Each pan-European shrine to lose its clientèle, then, some to rumour.

The divine no longer uncommon among things human:

That long-revered Black Virgin soon covered by a sack in the back of a
  white van.

207

Poem as *Jules et Jim*. Poem as *Hinz und Kunz*. But for what induced audience?

Absurdity of final truth—canary straight into dog's mouth?

Of course I desire fame even more: or bringing disorder to frame without
　　intrusion of reader and consequent thoughts of murder.

Best stay with lay figures for augurs to get by.

'Simple people' a resilient fable for example.

This is evidence by now and means mysteries, if not as Easter does.

A heavy crow breaks out of roadside bushes, keeping low.

208

This is a grim scheme and there will be some posthumous fuss.

Fascinating migratory raptors uncaring of our care; images reforming in
　　another—preferably archaic—air. Occasionally filmed from helicopters
　　while mating they readily scare.

Old poems cold paramours.

The dire drumming of forthcoming, that I cannot tire.

Acquired eloquent tears—first Patmore's, then ours.

Target-red November salvias marvellously spared—if challenged I shall count
　　on the Linnaean sign—so planted that the low-pitched autumnal sun
　　catches them briefly at ascent and decline.

Patmore should get about more: he and his 'perturbed moon of Úranus', his
　　rancour and hauteur, politics of the right; the echoes of young Milton
　　*contra tyranno*s in the odes; other similitudes by no means watertight.

209

Those razor-sharp high collars cutting into the under-chin—Coventry
   Patmore in a photograph is caught wearing one.
Paul Morel's brother was rumoured so to have died: erysipelas in the red
   raw-rubbed line. Folk were fragile then, even the colliers.
Bert Lawrence could scotch a girl's love as though in a village hall sketch of
   how not to behave.
The subsequential regard of men-of-letters (else appointed his betters); his
   seeming indifference to all such matters of reward; his exploitation of
   that one vulnerable chance, becoming fable.
It was ever thus in this nation, its animus incapable of fruition without dross;
   routine the pain and loss; blighted location.
'By whom and for whom I became a poet' is Patmore *in memoriam*, not quite
   going spare with memory and sorrow and, just possibly, shame.
I've seen but not read—I wish now that I had—a two-volume *Life*; and the line
   that confirms my theme—'perturbed moon of Úranus'—burns itself
   off with a particular flare like a natural gas that the latest workings no
   longer require.

210

'Is't England's parting soul that nerves my tongue?' Perturbed and part-
   disrobed, the line unstrung.
Hopkins, both tough and nesh, deplored Patmore's protestations as fetish:
   marital flesh, gentry nation; parody of the squire's code.
Ode as Tory tirade.
I admire the odd line that bears well its sign of purpose: entire and with an
   accomplished repose.
It is prosodic order, proud on the rim of its gyre, that bears the odd theme at
   any one time: a matter of stamina rather than of mood.

211

Poetry, tricky as nitrate to those who mistreat it, cannot be outwitted in its
    proper (many times now expropriate) field.
If I could I would of course parse my *ars poetica* on the ex-virginal face of a
    party election sticker.
But here my syntax is visibly (and audibly) breaking under pressure from a
    new window tax to fund untaxed national treasure.
There is somewhere here a mixed metaphor of sorts that I cannot placate,
    nor is there now any citizens' bureau where I might go to get it fixed by
    decent artisans at the expense of the state.

212

Yeats wrote about eating the human heart. I cannot believe that he ever gave
    the reality a thought. It is not at all like a cooked beet.
Poem as shapeless form in a sack.
Poem taking no part in the elementary scheme for fracking the back country.
The *Olney Hymns* may have gone too far towards extremis. But—
The Church of England today is a near-bankrupt holding company for things
    sacrosanct.
Severely bereft of Berkeley and Swift.
Johnson twinned 'thinking' with 'prudent' man; turned moral commonplace
    wiggy and strident.
He could not 'refute' the Ordinary of Cloyne by bruising his own foot against
    a stone.
But swallowed the cast-list of our distressed Island Story wherein the best and
    the worst appear lame.
The human heart that Yeats wrote about most likely a form of Brummagem-
    Indian charm.

213

I am dirtier now than an old man in Yeats's Irish theatre.

In the near-senile mastoid cavity an earwig of moist scar tissue regularly
appears, even after seventy years. By this time it may be mere grime.

When you write 'on a bit of newspaper' words meant to summon—what?—
one would assume that, should they fail, a scruff of the stuff might serve
to wipe your tail; as Leopold Bloom could have done to dispel his matu-
tinal travail and squatted coil.

We do well on the whole to unscramble continuity from tradition. Continuity
may be more important; the poem must affirm portent to make gravity
tremble.

214

Haecceitas appears out of black brickwork like evidence shallowly buried for a
hundred years. Dark remnants glim hallowly; there is a spontaneous
combustion in the vast bastion of waste.

The Church of St Francis Xavier, where Gerard was rebuked for overwrought
pulpit behaviour, I believe I could revere merely for his being (briefly) there.

Reconstructed to Dublin, poisoned iron drinking-fountain, finally even he
began to complain.

215

Gillian Rose presumed to compose four lines of 'gnostic' verse which, out of
respect, I will neither reproduce nor wholly erase.

It has to do with diremption as rat-eaten synonym: guilt as the taint of ignorant
intent; post-Shoah status of original sin as a well-documented continual
growing pain of the docile and inhumane.

'Strangers to ourselves as moral agents and as social actors', poets; and com-
pany directors; apprentices with slide rules and protractors; force fields
and plotted vectors; occlusion's patents; factors and regents; notorious
born-again saints.

216

Nineteen thirty-two is imbrued with my own blood.

I am not a Jew though I married one; and I subscribe to their iron scorn; *aude* Sandy Goehr, born in that same livid year.

Myself and my mother bled into each other; she was henceforth barren, I solitary; foreign to myself and dire to her.

The next immediate crisis—pyloric stenosis—was healed by acid and a glass rod: a method no-one since then has claimed to have undergone or understood.

217

Tristan Tzara, as with many an earlier explorer, out on his ear.

'The great lament over my obscurity' introduced no real parity.

The basilica of reason rears over the scene like any common obstacle

'Unshakeable lord ┆ unshakeable lord'.

218

'Chasing the dragon's tail' a perilous game in drably reckless Los Alamos at a time when even asbestos was believed beneficial, the climate stable: a cosmic mezuzah for fissionable material gone teledomestic.

'Poem as primitive form of cyberattack on the sanctity of the home.'

If poetry were as powerful even as that, I would gamble with my life at the same rate; but this is no such daemon or sprite. It does not make missile defence scramble nor investment recoil.

Los Alamos was never the Spirit of Poetry in Blake.

219

Toccatas perhaps gnostic. Drastic Stockhausen indubitably so. Your Camden
    Lock joss-stick, such conformable eccentricities, no go.
Alain-Fournier, thank heaven, did not live to venture to California. Isherwood
    and Huxley throve there heterodoxically for a time but without leaven.
And those whom they—dully, hysterically—inspired are part way through
    being themselves interred.
The horny shrubs that complained with the voices of the damned and dripped
    blood from their stubs even now react.
The shore-line is worked by those who under- and over-perform; who mime
    pleas to the ferryman as is expected of them.
All this makes for a queer interlude in my Gower-like screed: claims to
    intercalate error by re-enacting barbarous forms and alarums in a
    barber's mirror.
Dada successfully submits to the gnostic test of my disquiet's pudor.
I too am approaching the gates of exchange. Reach me that vinegar phial and
    small sponge; or some oil and cotton wool.

220

When my mother's mother was yet a tiny chiel, *Edwin Drood* had barely started
    to churn in the extravagantly-canny author's heady mill.
Middlemarch had not even begun; James was a young man with an untried but
    on-your-mark brain.
Poetry, I repeat, went (for that while) unserved by the great artery that joins
    theme to time and style.
Gerard, tipped fervent by the Birmingham Oratory, had made a burnt offering
    of his vatic temerity, and become creatively dumb.
Take any Hardy poem written when he was first smitten: how it fails to
    forethreaten what was to come.
My grandmother, I recall, read well, moving her lips silently the while; a nice
    brooch of purplish glass reflective on the bodice of her dark dress.

221

It may be, as you say, that there is a history to my kind of lumbering near-inert
    registry: the rhyming prose of that hermit Rolle in his snow-infiltrated
    spartan grove of holly.

Hard to verify: in English he was a sketchy bard; but I will take your word.

'Swet Jhesu, thy body is lyke a boke written al with rede ynke'—that's pretty
    good, I think. Pity about the rhyme.

Rolle unenticed, I imagine, by the wan-dark beauty of things delicately iced.

Dense holly trees are themselves a mystical experience, standing out against
    snow, as they so wonderfully do. Such visions, though, are mere elisions
    in time.

But not in all versions.

222

Diabetes is now affecting both eyes, though what this may symbolize I can't say.

'There's allus the wuk'us' was regularly said in the enclaves where we were
    bred; though among our own folk chiefly as an archaic rueful joke.

Geophysics' radar creates a desire for layouts of imagined original order. Some
    are beautiful: I would be glad of a couple for the wall or one on my easel.

Inventively consider: eventually our poverty falls to the highest bidder. Dead,
    I may thrive in your archive, let me presume, my name scanned in the
    general scheme of national illumination that's both bound and blind.

223

Had we been defeated and tied to the Nazi rote, Goebbels would have crowned
    Lord Haw Haw as poet laureate, probably in the Abbey, that prize
    sepulture of popular culture, eh?

Bowie had the best line with cliché after mine, disarticulating its artless
    continuity, taking it back into some single rudiment before the advent of
    too-coherent mass sentiment, its sweated industry.

His view of abridgements and segments, even so, was compromised by the
    milieu. He was a type of painless flagellant in the realm of language
    and song-rage: even though on the necromantic face of *Lazarus* he is
    posed in a style drawn from the files of that notorious old antic Dean of
    St Paul's.

224

A thirty-foot tapeworm, at enforced withdrawal, leaving its denture in the wall
of the large bowel: could this be at all real? Let me have my cerebral
spasm of drool.

Can recall, in Lewis's restaurant, Brum—last time before that terminator of a
bomb (we there on a rare jaunt)—a man with a crop of red grapes
sprouting from the integument behind one ear. I felt a chemical desire
to tug and caress that rubberoid mass: it has been a lifetime's obsession
I cannot explain; again I feel the saliva begin to run.

My nerves are erectile; my desires impractical; my self-will has been dissi-
pated; a shade like Aeneas I believe myself fated.

Is Dada, then, the abandoned Dido whom I mourn with sickening laurel and a
reeking urn; ex-subliminal but not here criminal; awaiting unforgettable
return?

How many, these days, respond to such a question with an orator's scotching
phrase?

225

It was to Brum that we rode *Midland Red* for a 'Hippodrome' pantomime.

I saw bright-polished shoes set level with my eyes in highlight window
displays.

To the same terminus I bussed white-faced for my French oral exam which, to
my shame, I but slenderly passed.

Between these events stately Victoriana was randomly bomb-reduced and slum
landlords were for a period deprived of their rents.

No longer spellbound I found it a hideous place, stranded on low-price high
Mercian heathland merely to erase mystery's heartland.

I had not then heard of Boulton and Watt or of the erudite Priestley set or
of the other élite such as John Baskerville; and I now accept that not
everything about that vast squat was vile.

Nor had Louis MacNeice come to my notice at that time, though already
I took a naive pleasure in verse provided that it ran to obvious metre
and rhyme.

226

When I confessed to the palely dressed lady that I had no testosterone I was
    prophesying, old son.
Does the moon inflict change? She appears without malice.
And my late nature is a *coup de théâtre* manufactured by dry ice.
Biological etiology, even, serves the Logos, the Word that survives vogues.
I cannot say to what this brings me or where it leaves me on any given day.
So many whom I admired are solidly interred [*points to his head*], each a
    vociferous similitude.
A shade too close to Leopardi, 'Chorus of the Dead', of which, fortunately for
    me, few here have even heard.
I believe I value BV as such as he deserve.
PS: The living likeness was due to a novel embalming fluid.

227

I've sat here, I fear, far too long, admiring Turing and becoming boring.
What for? For not quite singlemindedly winning the war—he had interests on
    the q.t.
The Manchester statue sets tat for piety, stranded on a kind of waste ground;
    though I doubt he would have much minded.
What he wrote, as boy and adolescent, of the ever-present spirit (in memoriam
    Morcom) moves me as does Berkeley on grammatical particles (look, my
    white knuckles!).
All my late poetry is here comprised as if there were no computerized crem,
    mortuary, legal or deterrent system even remotely in debt to him.

228

Parliament's clock tower pours thimbles of fine Puginry each time the cracked
    bell's enginry of whirliments rumbles the hour.
The collapse will be tragic, not vulgar; performed to a slow movement by Elgar.
No current denizen, not Corbyn even, will seem worthy of the nobly subsid-
    ing tune.
Pugin built for himself and for Christ's empire; and was therefore a kind of
    vampire.
Barry a subsumed half memory commemorate in summary.

229

The static exercise-bike in his basement next to a crammed wine-rack: such
    was my donnée, you might say, for that breakthrough elegy way back;
    and for an awkward fecundity since then.
For more than that dull reason I am in self-evident confessional season and
    mode. It was so provident I could barely speak, miming the astonish-
    ment, mining the fabulous lode without diminishment.
How introverted all this has become since I became self-narrated; even though
    the best of me is linear and simple: this present apology an example.
Poem as form found in a citadel of the mind if not exiled therefrom. To write
    thus is to proclaim a continuum, not a going rate.
For Gerard, 'summer's sovereign good' was swimming nude in the Hodder.
I know so well that same deep cleft; can tell how it might appear, a total recall,
    or near, to one, after-bereft, brinksman of despair.
Turing as victim of a public politic crime continues to draw me to its *drame*, as
    it must some others.
'The fury of intelligence baffled and inspired by circumjacent stupidity.' This
    needs to be felt through and through as prosody, though; and with the
    going rough.
Poem as problem for the 'concluding-problem': in this sequence a current
    theme.
No need to wring your carbolic-soaped hands every time.

230

That Congregational chapel seldom does marriage or funeral-bell. I have
    never there heard tell of ancient mariner or of 'loud bassoon'.
When the sun in winter sets down its low glinter the poorly made cheaply-
    tinted windows glow with the colour of Lucozade.
Grouse and racing pigeon can ignore the hen harrier of this region.
Such is the spoor of common opinion and sanctity of the gun.
Leopardi could put to good use this stark realm in slipped time: 'A se stesso'
    and 'La ginestra' and other *rime*.
In his writings he is profuse but not wordy; as indeed I try to be, whether or not
    I succeed.

231

'Semi-sentient force-field' spreads its indeterminate quotient of yield. If it
　　were true there would be some kind of break-through, some military-
　　style putting on the spot.

It may be picked up, as Yeats would say, from a bit of newspaper in the street;
　　or off a nail on a privy wall; and we know with what joy they gurn and
　　maul, those purveyors of ruin and rule.

Yeats's late disquiet that his thespian strut of rage had thrust those young
　　and of mid-age, into street and cage, was an uncalled-for caveat in the
　　partiality of those times and that state.

He required to be 'squired' and 'blooded', as perhaps he had seen an ill-starred
　　girl blooded at Lissadell; her response in some foxy way sexual and
　　undistressed.

Our words drive us into dishonesty by their own recalcitrance. That is but a
　　split root of the matter; and in such a strait as this few care whether we
　　are or are not practitioners of deceit.

The shiningly unleashed poem presents itself winningly, brushed, and in
　　admirable form like an Irish setter in and out of the frame or the gutter.

Well, then! The Easter Rising was not a popular cause but the luck of an élite,
　　guarantors of defeat to whom self-sacrifice was the penultimate ruse
　　that the English would fall for or rise to; as they reprise every last one of
　　such crises: for instance, Afghanistan.

Excuse my obviousness; and that type of standard refrain.

232

Wisdom, as hygiene, sure to touch its toes from time to time; even, though
    more rarely, the parts of shame.

Which were—are—so evident in Gandhi & Gandhi's India where the poor
    crouch briefly in a position of *postprandia*.

This memo to inform my present kind carer that we are *en route* to Tagore's
    ashram in Shantiniketan. Hardly the Grand Tour, even in memory.

At stations along the way I was served tea through the open window in recently-
    baked cups of rough clay that afterwards were to be broken, as though
    ritually, so it appeared to be.

We have, then, the collective motion of the train; and I have the singular
    demotion of my attestations to the divine.

But nothing so alien as now my body is, after—precisely—forty years, to the
    guarded passage of its exiled desires.

At Tagore's house they sang me a hymn and said it was by him. I found it, as
    I recall, hypnotically beautiful.

I also recall that I thought he had lived in some style. Everything indoors was
    (to my uneducated eye) tastefully regal.

Gitanjali, which in English is more or less on a level with *Songs of Travel*, won
    an early Nobel. Those who can read it in the original Bengali say it does
    'lovely things'.

'Ashram' most probably is the incorrect term for the estate I arrived at. It could
    have been a country gentleman's farm in the English shires. But I am
    accustomed to my brain as an entertainment of crossed wires which,
    as we tell ourselves, does no great harm.

But it does; it does. How glad I am, now, not to be in my own shoes.

Labyrinthine anatomy of the 'simply divine' understood by none.

233

To whom exactly must I become indebted in the foetid mêlée that may embar-
rass my demise; when shares in me possibly begin to rise?

Half a century ago we cheerfully made do with Whittle and Hoyle, VTL,
Jodrell Bank and the *Mail*; commanding forerunners to pursue; but our
flame of genius appears sunk, now that Dave Bowie has signed into the
tomb with his very considerable panache and aplomb.

It might be—or feel—good to invent a general creative *exeunt*, a second *Dunciad*:
to begin with civico-orphic courtesies parodied, not so much to embar-
rass some recent fatuous chat-laureate (*pace* MacDiarmid, majestic
rhetor and garrulous old soak) as to provoke the sheer bloody opportun-
ism of time to a tossed-in-passing valedictory remark.

234

Refulgent ruined sunflower with that mock black hole to your bent tower:

Eden and Elohim, 'a desire united them in one feeling of love'.

The Book of Baruch by the Gnostic Justin: I despair of ever getting the theology
of this thing checked-in and under repair.

Slowness to learn is in a large part redemptive, says the voice of the tempter.

Is it the brilliance of the pre-emptive that one would be wise to fear?

Hearing, yesterday, Toby Jones declare 'over the air' that he can weather, even
enjoy, a period of 'jeopardy', I conclude that he may be trapped in a bad
play (or film, possibly); and that what threatens is an irruption of com-
mon sense.

Poem as profoundly unemotional as a Purcell theme which is well into the
mathematics of pitch and time.

The dances of the spheres, I have already imagined, are without sentiment
towards our desires; but poetry takes absurd chances.

235

If this poem be a tower, its base a carrousel, I wish I had mastered Tarot while
I was still small and unwell.

In *Baruch* the third angel is a brute lacuna. From one angle it appears whole.
Fetch a torch though that may not help much.

Concentration I would set higher than fleshly compassion. But I speak rashly.

It is not true that a lust for metaphor engendered the Minotaur but as a
disincentive it will do.

236

Whales self-strand lately in North Sea shallows. We do not understand why.

The waters recede: neither covenant nor creed.

Seventeenth-century statesmen's obituaries are copiously tendentious even when they cite Grotius.

You'll say I am ungenerous to a necessary national *sagesse* of that time and place.

Poem in memoriam the Missing of the Somme: probably, as you claim, a misuse of the medium.

Just possibly in some extraordinary way worthy of them.

Scattered uncertain applause from both sides of the House of Mirth.

237

Poetry as both *Convention* and *Directory*, each with its terror factory of Greek scansion.

Most obituaries in this series fail to reach even the knees of the effigies whose achievements are such as to inspire wise travesties.

James Shirley carries it off very well; as does Lovelace who can imitate looking death in the face, serenely reinvigorating each poor commonplace of the lyre.

Nothing now seems thorough but what I can borrow for the benefit of this commonweal which holds the genius of England in its thrust and recoil.

A jejune sonnet to O.C. must not become a *sine qua non*. Not every poem a new imperium.

I cannot recall any caveat apart from that; though in my time I have seen broken and discarded claims scattered about, the oysters of poetasters.

238

'In Drumcliff churchyard...' but that's not Yeats borne stiffly shoreward
   toward the luminaries who are sadly lit: 'indomitable Irishry', claptrap
   and gaucherie; and everything vaguely accurst.

Yes, when I recall Sligo it is the dense wild fuchsia hedges that I see first.

To plot the aftermath of your own demise is unwise. Some can preclude the
   offence by attention to gaunt truth askance and gross word of mouth.

The bones might be anybody's from around Roquebrune. Not even the
   scruffiest could be interpreted as a deliberate slur on Eire and her
   catatonic civil war; but as a vision of fame not unlike Bottom's Dream;
   to that extent arguably beneficent, where the dominions merge, like the
   wild fuchsia hedge, resplendent in wind-surge, redresses omens.

239

Petty complaint being the fulcrum around which swing the twin energies of
   attainder and perilous affront.

Poem as one case of post partum depression, in some part with cause yet
   without reason.

Take cigarette-etiquette in the old black and white B movies:

The donor of the first cylinder has his own lit by the recipient; it appears
   a point of honour and either class- or self-discipline however quaint it
   may seem to us. A female smoker is like a clever novice at snooker.

Poem as item of Greek Fire, then; the expensive, choosily-used purifier.

The scuffed tectonic plates of imagination rarely create a decisive station for
   the nation's variegates;

Though even now your transported clan stand on the moon and warble bar
   parlour hits, like someone's gran in the Blitz.

Matter is meaningless in the absence of spirit, said or says McTaggart whom
   gifted boy physicists once read and who is long dead and vaguely noble.

While almost all that you once covertly revered has by now reappeared
   worldwide as an infamous cartoon: a woman with a spittoon.

240

'A brain with canine teeth'—the late Gottfried Benn who enhances my creative
    trances to the power ten.
In the impending referendum I shall vote to remain, *Canaan* notwithstanding, in
    which I derided the Maastricht Treaty as an international corporate fraud.
The alternative now is an England of rotten boroughs and Hobbits *maudits*.
In the deepest sense I have never changed my mind.
If, henceforward, all that we have to sustain our pride is a form of hit-or-miss
    solitary genius, there is not a chance that collective board-room intransigence
    will get us through. The Vulcan was a marvel of a plane, though that has
    been long gone; and I fail to recall, since then, much else of worth.
'A brain with canine teeth': you can't touch a certain kind of German hound
    for crowding in on the death even if muzzle-bound; nor should poetry's
    energy derive from a needy urge to teach, nor even from some deeply
    satisfying, half-hidden yet flagrant wound.

241

Poetry's origin as chief brain-surgeon to the sacred authorities in the execution
    of their mysteries, wise up to: I have a notion it is like fate.
Do there need to be signals of my indebtedness outside the mock-security
    of code?
Orchestrated Westminster chimes to give warning of things fated, as when that
    telegram was delivered to three-storied staid 'Mahim' at eleven a.m. on
    Armistice Day, for example; the worst betrayal of pitiable hope in local
    record and portrayal.
From now on the gutters will always overflow and all correspondence received
    by that family will be written on enamel.

··

The fall in the value of agricultural tithe constrains the call to undertake
    agronomic scholarship hardly at all.
Depression may have wrought the demography of *A Shropshire Lad* more than
    we once thought it had: short of the ready for beer and baccy and
    half-decent bread; taking the Queen's unfailing shilling; at their most
    becoming when dead.
All the more credit to them who yet 'stride amid the gleam' and are never at a
    loss for a rhyme.

··

There is no Ironbridge Gorge in Terence's elegy; and why Clun should be so
 quiet he begrudges time to explain; though on Uriconium and Roman
 exaction he is *au fait*; and in the fluent beauty of Teme, rather than that
 great artery of a neighbour river, he has, as critics say, secured his theme.
Tory Old Believer that he is: his grandfather at Catshill burying and blessing
 my sweated, berated and branded kin.

242

Purple the most readily legible colour in a poor light, as Coastal Command
 navigators quickly learned—unless this was a cruel leg-pull all around.
Of little use to castaway Ravilious, such advice. Gone down off Iceland seventy
 years and still not found. Never mind; though war-artist commissions
 commonly that kind of offhand, even when not designed to patronize
 and offend.
Between subservience and subversiveness, then; though for me to maintain
 this line of attack may be a lost cause running slack.
No consequence immeasurable here and now to the minor outriders of small
 fame, war-poet Vaughan's spiritual providers; progenitors and inheritors
 of his dark, coded rhyme. The anxious navigator with his intercom.
Ravilious a shade supercilious merely to share overall blame? No sign or token
 of that on the unbroken oceanic swell above which the gremlined
 Hudson ran out of time.

. . . .

Now that I no longer swim, rhythm is not my *te deum*.
The funeral sentences are here less an act of homage than a *collage* requital of
 collateral damage.
Vatic one-liners *in memoriam* should not be sclerotic deposits of shame.
Dyslexic *mores* essential, nay vital, if we are to rediscover and rename our
 personal stars before all this is over.
Professor Brian Cox may be older than he looks, than the adolescent fixture of
 his fizzy talks.
Set up my own renegotiable stable of torch-songs from dire to feeble?

. . . .

Poem as a form of pseudo-mimesis reduced to mere numero-cursus yet still able to handle its own reverses, and re-rehearse. Bless rather than curse according to revised fable.

Subversiveness well-aired *in re* old Chris, even at the memorial rental service; there is very little that cries out to be omitted or referred. *Memo*: rehire; either in parts or entire.

Whether these are questions more of existence than of cadence...

Canaan indeed canine: at last on record that has been precisely stored.

Great poet staked out at the spot like a tethered goat. For what?

243

Is it necessary even now to explain my Anglophone cult of Benn? Not Hilary, that cultivator of mental celery. Gottfried is the one I mean.

Coarse-prissy Nazi also-ran, he was not a 'nice man'.

Complicitous that austere 'inner exile' of the 'good' *Wehrmacht* officer.

The army, we are told, was sealed off from the *einsatzgruppen* operating far to the rear. Don't even for a moment believe that; though, had I stood there, my mouth would have been stopped as with a gob of cement by fear.

Had the general staff itself stood naked beside a mass grave, each with a child in his arms that he could not save, Abdiel would have descended amid flames; there ought to have been millennia of magical sums in decent Romania and the golden Ukraine.

Parataxis, let us be clear, angers the grammatically austere; they hear it as a sort of *koax-koaxis*. Linguistically Benn was a type of carnal puritan, austere of praxis, his *topoi* noxious.

There is no denying what 'up-to-date' may supplicate in the long term or the short spate of assaying.

Such a verset is about the bearable extent of a particular line of wit; its posited capacity to pass without detriment to the sign.

Hapax legomenon neither too late nor too soon.

My apology for an epilogue postponed *sine die*.

Poem as pre-emptive strike that no qualm hinders; like 'every field commander's dreams'.

244

How close one gets lately to *The Mirror for Magistrates*; five hundred years or
  thereabouts of European polity with which *poesis* binds itself to engage
  in the various kinds; and which is set down in the guise of a thesis on
  metempsychosis not unrelated to John Dee's; and which once meant a
  fair deal to people more belligerent and intelligent than us.

A period hereabouts would not come amiss.

Once I swam over the lair of a snapping turtle; later, struck numb, watched it
  briefly appear, its body like an overturned scuttle of plated metal.

This was in Walden Pond, at the wild end. I did not revisit. I have never been
  comfortable with Thoreau, his desire to go right up to Nature and
  amaze her.

What else—pike-jawed and as deep-browed as Ted—can I persuade to engage
  and endorse my lately obsessive attitude?

245

'At the juncture of chalk and fen'—a petty fixation of mine—the style and
  staple of school 'readers' from about nineteen ten on.

I can do as little as you to explain whence we were drawn or where we shall
  have gone in short order (my mother, now almost sixty years' earthen
  bone, vamping a Woolworth's sheet of 'South of the Border' on our
  toneless piano).

And I have ever been in a form of sun-haze or rain-squall limbo, driven passive
  as I am through learning and mourning to the urinous dissavour of wild
  allium, this according to some primal rite, further adorning the nation,
  its moral taste long ago vitiated by *The Wicker Man* or some other dance
  marathon.

All that is imperfectly fictive has been tenaciously addictive; and goes towards
  most people's idea of a famous film I presume.

My slowly deteriorating brain is in daily-nightly competition with something
  it has long believed its own, and as steady as Orion in popular star-lore.

The plastic uterus of commercial good will still gives me the jitters; though
  nothing drastic and in spite of which I continue to perform well.

246

The copious lost property of our best poetry, then and now...

Will Brangwen at Lincoln Cathedral: an 'original': signifies type rather than it
    does origin; whose template is far from ideal; who is touchy and refrac-
    tory which, for Lawrence, always implies something of the male virgin
    principle that prematurely dies.

Every phrase, you may observe, is a course correction between reality and
    fiction: I do not here mean failure of nerve.

More, even, than with *Areopagitica* ('*encore encore*, sixteen forty-four'), the
    harvest that 'whitens' without self-travesty may appear to some the
    semantics of novice titans stuck amid bitumens.

Helpless within history the maker whelps *mea culpa*'s, feral blood and mastery.

247

An old man dying in the bed opposite appears to be lying in his best state; it is
    like the scant funeral of American Civil War general left unattended on
    a studio lot.

I am not myself a mourner, unless observance matches observances.

He will be gone in an hour or a little more; and I will return to my book on
    Brady the photographer.

The absence of a curtain does not to my mind harm deportment, though I am
    no connoisseur. I would not desire 'privacy' at this time as if dying were
    an act of shame.

We are confused by the obligatory because we so desire our own story and have
    so sure a sense of just fame as opposed to notoriety.

248

Repeat: act of dying no shame in these circumstances—the powers of darkness notwithstanding, and our offences.

Even so, I will have omitted some consideration; instance, the next-of-kin do not like it done in this fashion.

Bloody next-of-kin, what do they know about it? This is not neglect nor is it exposure of an ignoble cull which briefly held us in dismay with our fellow rabble.

As my memorial, even so, I should be glad to let fall some phrases from *Urne Buriall* or Harvey's latest edited *Circulation of the Blood*, as though these were generally and recurrently understood, not things the Commonweal makes light of as we go under 'for good' (some even now—the impenetrable—doubt we will).

249

Scope of popular English heroic poem the same as that of the Big Top.

If the poetry is any good, I mean; as I believed *Reynard the Fox* to be when I was twelve or thirteen. It was, and still is, a demonstrable success if the old voice is capable.

My piano compositions failed because I could not compose a convincing ground bass.

'When I survey the wond'rous Cross' has the best bass line in English hymnody. Even better than Tallis's 'third mode' tenor, I'd say.

There was yet enough gross in the verbal mass to let me presume I was at last 'called' to deploy verse; though it was a loser's choice, one that I lament to this day.

250

Lupercal: a clownish ceremony about which to play donnish.

Origin of the Purification of the Virgin.

Honoured the she-wolf who had reared the cast-off twins on Rome's behalf.

Ted had an urgent sense of what England needed; its genius re-emergent, myth-readied.

Blood smeared on the forehead; women symbolically gored. You could so read it; obscure omen.

Latterday Casaubon; nation of ancient carbon.

....

The devil gets into us when we are portentous, though not only then.

No real struggle against the natural throes of the surreal?

....

It is the rare poem that reaches full term. Massive the haplessness, the going spare. *Lupercal* noble enough in its interim of common foible, vulnerable as a capercaillie, or hare from the stubble.

251

Occasional the passing bell; even so a massive proclaiming.

Sometimes a quartertone's insistence that I do not understand so well.

Part of the English rite that even now has the strength of writ.

Shakespeare's rumour-bearers to the nation are part of that same tradition:

Alongside pseuds' tolerance where power presides over due tolerance for power:

The treachery in Gaultree if we wish to keep it rural:

Or the Rising in the North where only the betrayed are on oath:

And skin-of-his-teeth Skelton holds court in *The Garland of Laurel*.

252

My diction having metastasized into the cheerily odd, I doodle with a
    tattooist's needle several things I would once not have said, let alone
    addressed on parade.

Whether poetry is unreal is best tested by using it to settle a hotel bill.

It could well have a radical clout and be slid into the till by a good sport
    awaiting some remote victory-shout.

Again the apple in full flush, again the fretty-leaved lime.

The half-accustomed acceptance of mythical time.

Three weeks or so out of that clash with delirium in the old men's crèche.

The implication so far is that there is somewhere a final equation:

As Péguy must have believed and, in his own fashion, proved as a type of
    sublime fiction.

253

If testimony is of a witness how should I summon or speak for myself?

So short the time while the lime leaves have become denser and darker.

'Il Penseroso' is my cynosure here. I my own eyesore.

Poetry is not a natural lapse of divinity through the lips.

Nor does it now resemble what Pindar gathered on his memorandum slips.
    A Pythian ode could not afford to list prize-winners in the wrong order
    or mismeasure their leaps.

The discourtesy of history is like the debasement of money. Don't say you
    heard that first from my chastened quips.

Pindar, I bow to him, held the right trim between riot and decorum. Mere
    inspiration I will not now pass judgement upon.

Such triumph of human exhaustion in this inexhaustible piston.

The back garden apple has blossomed beyond even last season's generous
    burden and span. Its life and mine I re-imagine coterminous, though
    missing some harmonies.

The final bar of Schubert's *Quintet* is not a sigh but an exultant snarl.

254

It is the pragmatics, permit me to say (who am rawly beaten by Pythagoras to this day), that sort us out. Poetry is the art of the knout.

In my father's time I worked rhyme against form with smears of poisonous blue indelible pencil. He also let me part-expend my rage on any leftover blank page of a 'surplus' police notebook; my lips of purple slake.

He was a good man; I brought him pain and pride.

When he abruptly died greed obliterated the 'citizen's code'. His pitiable wallet disappeared before or during the brief ambulance ride.

Nietzsche's 'mysterious hieroglyph linking the state and genius' feeds on my father's brain as well as mine (and my great grandfather's, the Welsh furnace-man). I cannot explain.

Mass migration renders all things obsolete except onward motion. Devotion and loving candours mostly it squanders, and all connection; and just and unjust fraction.

255

The German *Widerstand*, now but not then much in demand, saw themselves as the secret *type* of a redeemed Deutschland.

In late November last year I laid my pretty and costly wreath under the iron bar from which they had straitly hung in grubby Plötzensee, NW of Moabit where Emil's adventures had been set.

So little of broad general good came of their spirit. Even if they had taken power, Maastricht would have stood unveiled on the hour; and barely more than a semitone apart from the trumpets of the Thirty Years War.

Take heart, the Funeral Sentences are neither an act of homage nor a bill for damage.

256

Notice how comfortably unsettled I become, the more this sequence is revealed
    as my real home. With always an encyclopedia on which to rest my left
    arm, I do not have to resort overmuch to erm.
I wrote against Maastricht on that first occasion and believed I had done well
    by appealing to a modern Passion.
In 'De Jure Belli ac Pacis' they stood invoked: those few who had worked for
    Germany's overthrow because it had become a Satanic state.
'Vexilla regis' I named the aegis of all secular harmonies.
There is a rhetoric of 'endless choice' (Sedley) in Purcell's court carapace
    which saddens me. No irrefutable evidence of cosmic cadence emerges
    save as tonal mirages.
I mean, I am distressed by an ostentation of second best which may have
    metastasized the nation into a form of self-arrest.
Purcell's majesty is aloofly engaged in fretting away what was probably meant
    to have him upstaged in transfixed jest.
Great music is always strikingly managed and maged; great poetry not: many
    times this moves queerly, fails its own plot.
I enter these as a memo, an item of note, barely camouflaged.

257

The paradox of vision; the oxymoron of mere omen.
You say I fail to engage the ordinary language of men and women.
'These are they who when the saving thought came shot it for a spy'—*The
    Orators*, which I would now so esteem my rare wit to have written at that
    time in the nation of deprivation and dinky tourers.   ·
But I compromise the citation; the speaker is himself one of ill passion, an
    abuser of position, inverter of *mores*.
Auden said later that he wrote out of a state of confusion, touched by matters
    illiberal and ill-bidden.
Did he think the generations would care for his gnomic recantations, convene
    debates comparing his political bad manners with those of Yeats; treat-
    ing these things as though they were not futile?
Well, so they did, marginally and for a while. And it was a pitch as good, I believe,
    as some have since decreed in the retrospective, part-retroactive, mood.
When I was little I read the *Daily Mail*; and believed that a chosen few were
    born to rule: like, yet unlike, Dryden, Purcell, and their 'Fairest Isle'.

258

To say 'Eliot should have quit, still the out-of-line pierrot, in nineteen twenty-
eight' is less than adequate even if we are agreed he was no hero.

I am in a mood to berate, my attitude a mode of fetishism.

The cyclic structure I try to maintain is like *Lear*—the 'wheel of fire' which
does not, as some suppose, equate mere sexual desire so much as impacted
soul-fate, self-generated in great part, with the base infinitude of our lot.

Eliot treats this in the fourth *Quartet* which derives from Yeats's study of various
fiats that afflict one who writes, though not just anybody who does so.

Not you and your prize buzz-saw, I ought to say.

I have never been a good strategist, due as much to inhibitions as incompetence.

If you say 'tactics' I think immediately of motorcycle racetracks circa nineteen
forty-six when Britain was in a dire fix; the screech and glare at Perry Barr.

Though an outsider to most things I did far more than stare. I caught modes of
speech among taut nerve-strings, the odd stridency of a match-head's flare.

At thirteen, even, I had this remonstrance to prepare.

259

With debts insoluble as some nineteen nineteen war reparation the banks
have again faced down the nation. At once amassed and dissolute, the
account is cast.

Britain in supposed stupor is to fill the heel of a giant spoor, having the
proportions of a super-dinosaur-state pensioner.

Earlier, Coleridge and Ruskin inscribed their honest and good-hearted error:
the new Britain to emerge like a bride from the Book of Esther while
they sat, somewhat as Mordecai 'in the king's gate'.

Carlyle was ever a malign twister, clad awhile like Nestor.

These no doubt merely the smoke and mirrors of my debt.

'My ridiculously beautiful wife' and other clichés from the crown of life; all the
common parlance of sincere dalliance and sexual affiance; wedding euphoria,
the Soria Moria of popular pleasances, brass band at the lych gate.

The rectitude of a generational structure plus the national architecture;
dereliction of small farms and great houses, silly light fiction, con-man
and bitch, fresh emphasis upon the aitch.

'Tragic and sentimental purification' wrote Keynes in a footnote, also of
nineteen nineteen, addressing himself to no particular nation, 'which in
some degree will relieve its harshness'—as though his panoramic gaze
were like Vishnu's.

260

The Peaky Blinders were High Tory handlers and minders, riders to hounds, *agents provocateurs* for contrived wars, dealers in contraband armoured cars, playing off White against Red: and all within twelve miles or so of where I was bred in the agrarian-industrial watershed of north-east Worcestershire: *The Land of Smiles*, Ansell's Ales, suchlike lingering dwales. Innocence and evil over my head, though I was libidinously preoccupied with thoughts of the devil in that marred childhood of which I am both ashamed and proud.

Should you conclude how my historico-clerical sense is in overload remember that I am agitating a cyclic pindaric ode. The leverage pin, I say again, is nineteen nineteen; a century either way across that line will serve my *oeuvre*, provided I keep my nerve.

Jokes that appear to run amok may have been bespoke.

The non-adept can sometimes adapt: bad writer great dynamiter; though that will be rare and though I do not write primarily in order to make you disappear.

261

'High Tory', no doubt, will have you in stitches and fury; but I know what I am about.

Your Peaky Blinder was your basilisk or salamander.

Tory, to me at this latter day, is both rabble and oligarchy.

The well-reimbursed iron fist Italianate condottiere; Sir John Hawkwood was one. The Peaky Blinders could have been his men.

Tell me it is an incomprehensible label so to apply.

Coleridge and Ruskin, my mind's heroes, were high Tories:

Yeats with his night-dogs, torched Furies and Blue Shirt marching programme:

Pound's two 'Italian Cantos'; his cerebral pogrom; his readiness to play court fool at Mussolini's foot-stool:

Original division, ultimate diffusion or fusion in whoomph creation, repeated as demeaning legends of anthropomorphic Fall, no matter now how minuscule to the new scale.

I once heard a good sermon on that from a certified clerical wise woman denied preferment.

Such passion we put into being dispassionate: is that reasonable?

Poem strung from the keeper's gallows at All Hallows among other vermin, as may be seasonable.

262

In the beginning was the Big Bang creating *yin* and *yang*, and many another
lively and deadly dialectical thing.

The last 'steady state' delegate has retired for the night. I have inquired, at the
gate, of an inebriate guard.

That there is strong correlation between character and fate is probably proven
somewhere.

If so, our nation in nineteen forty was a major exception to that rota: in the past
year both braggart and cringing under Pathé's star.

A massive redistribution of moral weight, with something as small as a
threepenny bit poising the scale, had us prevail.

Whether such matter could penetrate a black hole and survive is not now
possible to tell; given the riven data of eternity and the relative equanimity
of heaven.

'Turbo-capitalism' encourages fatalism.

263

Rabbits will attack stoats; it is as if desperate peasants were savaging
landsknechts. I cannot make much of this but it is good to watch.

An allegorical metaphor is forming that I must dispatch as unbecoming.

Not one of us has ever surprised Hobbes in his intellectual burrow with
breaking news of some unexpected terror, non-ruminant though he was
and non-combatant in the wars.

Poets are sometimes like rabbits, sometimes like stoats.

My Staple Hill origin is texted 'illiterate' as late as eighteen sixty-nine. I have
told you this and shall probably spread the word again before I lose control
of my brain and my pen.

Such reprise somewhat like the bread poultices with which my frantic mother
once scalded both my scabbed knees that had 'taken bad ways'.

264

I meant, of course, in my recent allusion to *Lear*, that sex-spoilure is not an
autonomous evil but an indivisible part of a malign hemisphere (which
is what 'Thou art a soul in bliss' implies).

My apologies, therefore, for not making that clear.

Some who reposition this theme seem to believe that they are conducting a
Victorian mission for seamen.

Or it becomes a generational cultural thing like the far-ebbed vogue for a
dialogue song by Sonny and Cher.

To say of *Lear* that its 'spiritual character throws a singular light upon our
landscape' is to distort Scholem, a mind updated from that of a medieval
Jewish Schoolman.

The 'landscape' that I refer to is a dimension of virtue which has never been
an unquestionable part of common nature.

That we can so misalign is one of those deep-rooted nationalist sentimentalities
that seem to do little harm in 'where to stay' commentaries (that could
even reclaim *Animal Farm*).

. . . .

Come June I shall vote 'Remain' though disquieted by what I know will even
then, even if we win, squat in the high seats, acting as if benign albeit of
covert reign.

265

Do I possess what you term a 'heightened imagination' as the norm?

I who alter, more than thirty years later, 'blood' to 'gleet' because the field
where he fell was, and remains, sugar beet; and one must align invention
with those particular stains?

I seem to become more like an old time bank-teller with his near-immoveable
celluloid collar, sweating to account for a mislaid small denomination
coin, keeping at it through the precious Saturday afternoon; more from
dread of dismissal than through loathing of error.

It was a garrison nation infiltrated by agents of far-fetched guerison: share
Gerard's prayers for the eternal joys of better-off-dead bugler boys.

Heightened imagination is not exaggerated fancy: that is necromancy.

And, really, I have small patience with the 'white radiance' school though I do
not at all blame Shelley.

266

I look at the handsome intelligent face of Stephen Lawrence, and mourn; and
     at the coarse blebbed features of his murderers, and feel shame.

The virtues attributed our nation are a Referendum scam, as with misinter-
     pretation of *A Midsummer Night's Dream*, or 'Jerusalem' or the nuclear
     deterrent or Classic FM or the Heir Apparent.

Drenched Queen Salote in her topless barouche was without doubt winner of
     the popular vote; yet the solemnity of the occasion, as we viewed it on
     a haughty neighbour's set, was in no way demeaned by her joyous and
     generous panache.

Even so, missionary-stew jokes were soon on the go among those po-voiced
     who, behind the scenes, ran the show or were otherwise privileged
     commentators on the ancient black and white runes.

I am like the 'Great Eastern' attempting to lay cable; the exertion palpable, the
     outcome feeble. My stupefied conclusion is that something effectual
     should come my way—'not a KBE'—for the strenuosity of pre-acoustic
     exhortation.

But this is not actually how things are now done here, even though you may
     have advanced your own vocation in this year of scrambled floatations.

I look at the beautiful intelligent features of Stephen Lawrence and mourn.

I inspect the clam-stares of his murderers and recognize how haplessly jejune
     I am; my preening morality a spell of keening garrulity.

I stand appalled at the threshold of the eternally miscalled.

267

All that lying and spying and false witness: it takes one's breath that Wyatt's
     was a natural death.

Such lyricism of early demise for which immortality was, indeed is, the prize.

Such long fingernails scratching the gut of a ready-to-hand lute, toying with
     treason's entrails, I can readily comprehend, though very little beyond
     that, humming, in my own *sotto voce*, an unprivileged note.

Henry the Seventh's earlier perjury in the coronation proclamation established
     a fashion and an obsession and has lately been much written upon.

Permit me now to be a trifle enigmatic. This is still a ridiculous and a danger-
     ous trade-topic.

Poem as groom of the stool, both privileged and foul; addressing the nation's
     unwiped *cul*.

'Poet spared death sentence' (*Guardian*). But not through any petition of mine.

268

Believe, now, my odes are a form of 'oppositional defiance disorder', a trendy term.
Suggest something else, that may strike you as true or just as effectively false?
An icon needs to be more than a mere stick-on memo of Nemo.
Poem programmed to triumph in injury time. That has a ring to it and does
    not, moreover, overweight a quote.
'Stuprate' I got wrong lifelong and will have to rewrite. But barely possible
    after eighty, I should have thought, despite 'blood' to 'gleet'.
So amateurishly lies the head of him appointed by comedy to feign dead.
To suppose hegemony hierarchy: is not that the root of our woes?

269

'Futures' a term of hypothetical values, cash-sutures.
No-one speaks of the 'future of poetry' any more.
The term was 'in' when such as Christopher Caudwell and Julian Bell were
    self-immolating for Spain.
It's about time that we looked at them again.
Not, of course, from any desire to restore Marxism to the intellectual poor; but
    to find once more reason and emotion in the same span of structural
    imagination.
Caudwell deplored the lost 'public value' of the word; or maybe he noted it
    simply for the record.
At five this was not something I had thoroughly explored though, as I recall,
    I must even then have caught something of Caudwell's mood:
Much as I caught impetigo of the *regio* in the contagious Fairfield school-yard.

270

Oligarchical nation. Arbitrage still the rage? Pseudo reparation sometime to emerge? Relation of language to things at large?

Contretemps through compromise: sooner or later my stumps would have marched on your thighs. Like that man at Otterburn? Yes.

How's this for a style, arbitrator of how much makes a mile, Mercator versus village debater?

Success hardly an issue, somewhat to my original surprise.

Professionalism a means of controlling spasm; but avoid truism.

On the day that we betray our souls finally to the cartels, we may be just about ready for *The Second Mrs Tanqueray*: arbitration by the well-made play, even though few revivals for rave's co-aevals.

Self-referential theism hagiography of schism, as in nineteen sixty eight, variously rehearsed of late. Let me here further state:

That the Chancellor is author of the narration barely to be put to the motion; to the nation, rightly, had I such power:

Otherwise there are the inside pages that alone carry the burden of our suffrages:

Stadia that come alive only at behest of the media.

Tele-perspectives work in such a way that a goal kick vanishes into ancient history, a potent speck.

No poem wholly opium of the people: not even McGonagall or *Howl* or the kenotic verses of St Paul, or Ovid's on Baucis and Philemon, that exemplary old couple. Even on this scale there are deposits that repel us to unrequital.

271

The numbness after the shock of exit, big-bummed Britannia in her tracksuit; her phantom lap of honour; no other runner.

July the dark month; the lime leaves turned matt. The newly-bloomed mallow will see us re-autumned before it falls fallow.

Even so, the power of stout roses has risen watt by watt against the afterglow of each brief thunder-shower.

EDITORIAL NOTES

Geoffrey Hill planned *The Book of Baruch by the Gnostic Justin* as a posthumous work, to consist of as many poems as he would live to complete. He composed the book in three stages. First, in rough-draft notebooks, he worked phrases and sentences into verses and drafts of poems; second, in fair-copy notebooks he wrote out whole poems; and third, I produced at intervals new typescripts incorporating additional photocopies from the fair-copy manuscript plus corrected pages from the previous transcript. At each stage Hill made a large number of revisions, some definitive, some tentative.

At his death Hill had revised and corrected sections 1–226 of the typescript. On these pages, he left a few dozen additional revisions and queries which we did not discuss before his death. In the main text I have adopted without comment his definitive corrections and revisions (usually made in pen and accompanied by a strike-through of the text to be altered). I transcribe below Hill's more tentative comments. In a few instances, he made changes to the fair copy without also adding them to the corrected typescript. I have incorporated these changes.

In the fair-copy notebooks, the additional, untranscribed poems bring the total number to 271. In the final rough-draft notebook, a few additional verses, presumably to be added to section 271, appear nearly finished; these I have transcribed below.

The section numbers of the typescript do not correspond to the fair-copy notebooks because some of the poems were deleted or transformed into several new sections at the typescript stage. The numbering of the typescript has been taken as final, although Hill queried this on a few occasions in the typescript.

The copy-editing of this volume followed the principles used for *Collected Critical Writings* (2009) and *Broken Hierarchies* (2014) except that I have not sought to introduce the same degree of editorial consistency.

Hill's comments on the poems

45.7 lathering her spurs] On the typescript, Hill altered 'slathering' to 'lathering'. He wrote in the margin: 'MS has "slathering". Talk to Ken'.

123.28 Hill wrote in the margin 'differs from NB1 p. 88' in the margin of the typescript. The manuscript (NB1) reads:

> The harm is not yet any place where I might step aside to dice, though by now an item in the parallel cosmos where Lucullus, a triumphal general, is hurled into nothingness even from the gates of hell—that first-prize-winning display at the last Railwaymen's Ball.

128.9 pisses this time serenely] Both the typescript and fair-copy notebook read 'this time pisses serenely'. On the typescript, Hill indicated in pencil that 'this time' and 'pisses' might be transposed, noting in the margin 'Ask Ken see nb1, 126'.

149.15 knew Dodford] On the typescript, which reads 'I knew Dodford well', Hill circled 'knew' in pencil and crossed out 'well'; in pen he circled the whole phrase 'I knew Dodford well'. In the margin he wrote 'NB' and referred to the fair copy notebook (p. 108) where he also deleted the adverb 'well'.

195.5 pet form of wet psoriasis. Call the vet.] Hill wrote 'set' in pencil over 'pet' and added the sentence 'Call the vet' at the end of the line. He wrote in pen a double vertical line in the right margin. I print the additional 'Call the vet' while keeping the original 'pet'.

199.3 desk lid as I have earlier described.] The typescript originally ended with 'desk lid'. Hill struck through the final period and added 'as I have previously said'. On the fair-copy, he struck through the period and added 'as I have earlier described'. I print the addition as given in the fair-copy notebook.

Hill's draft additional verses to the final poem

I spy Lorelei of mute patriotic song (say) horridly offering her irrational salute
    to the worst calamity that has struck the nation since that first day of the
    Somme affray: if you will please pardon my locution, representing as it
    does the ill-done-by, whose bloodymindedness, equal to any amount of
    abuse, aims once and for all to be boss.

Thus we self-abort in maladministered trance and become an offense to our-
    selves and our neighbours.

We shall undergo Sisyphean not Herculean labours.

....

Summum imperium (Bodin) recovers its meaning in time as in some formal
    garden, which cannot be merely arrangement of metre and rhyme.
    Whether this would mean Sissinghurst and the National Trust is difficult
    to forecast. I would have it secured by rhyme as by royal brevet.

What sovereignty means is ink instantly dry.

Whether such a term as *summum imperium* can illuminate an art form when it
    evidently carried weight in the Referendum I would doubt, but employ
    it anyway, as harbouring a type of specious authority which some
    might equate with moral bearing as they might these grand rose-heads
    uprearing or the traditional glamour of laurel.

....

How do I rate? Anything disordinate in that?